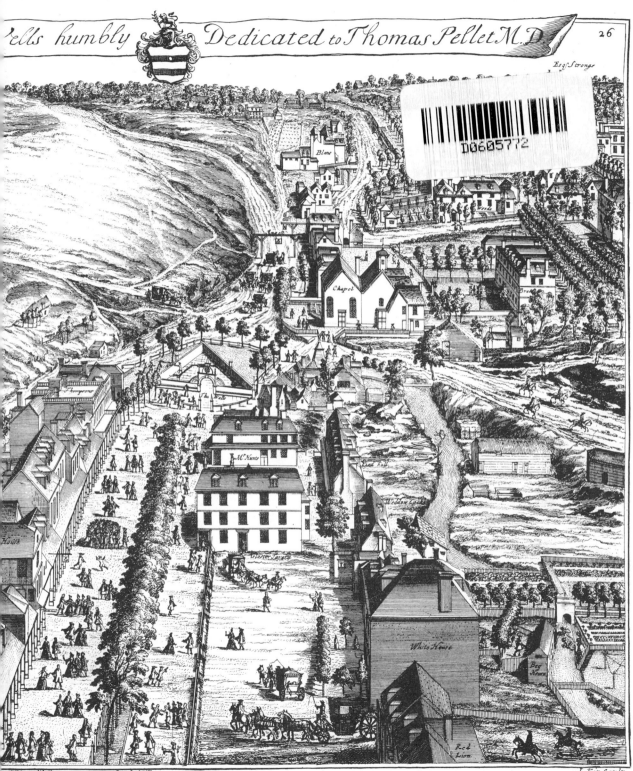

ells humbly Dedicated to Thomas Pellet M.D.

Esq.Strange

Blass

Chapel

Thompson

Mr.Keate

Glover Layer

White House

Red Lion

Uper Walk   Lower Walk   I Kip Sculp.

ROYAL
TUNBRIDGE WELLS

A Pictorial History

The dippers: Mrs. Chatfield on the left and Mrs. Mercer on the right are continuing the tradition started three hundred years before by the legendary Mrs. Humphreys, who assisted Lord North when he sowed the seed of the future town of Tunbridge Wells by his discovery of the spring in 1606.

ROYAL TUNBRIDGE WELLS

A Pictorial History

Roger Farthing

Phillimore

1990

Published by
PHILLIMORE & CO. LTD.
Shopwyke Hall, Chichester, Sussex

ISBN 0 85033 750 X

Printed and bound in Great Britain by
BIDDLES LTD.
Guildford, Surrey

To Sylvia

List of Illustrations

Frontispiece: Edwardian dippers

Illustration Acknowledgements

Grateful acknowledgement for permission to use illustrations (not to mention assistance often beyond the call of duty in finding and providing copies) is due to: the Tunbridge Wells Museum and Art Gallery for nos. 8, 20, 21, 25, 28, 34, 42, 43, 50, 62, 63, 65, 66, 70, 74-77, 80-84, 88, 91, 93, 98, 107, 111, 124, 126, 128-30, 133, 134, 136, 137, 139, 140, 144-46, 149-51, 157, 161 and 162; Tunbridge Wells Reference Library for nos. 6, 11, 16-18, 59, 99, 104-06, 108, 110, 114, 116, 117, 120, 123, 125, 135, 142, 147, 148, 152, 154, 155, 158, and 159; Kent Archives Office, Maidstone, for nos. 24, 36, 37, 44, 45, 78, 97, 100, and 101; the National Portrait Gallery, London, for nos. 2, 14, 15, 30, 38, 40, 41, 52, 53, 55, 67, 69, 102 and, with individual thanks to Judith Prendergast, 132; the British Library for nos. 7, 9, 10, 47-9, 64, 112 and 113; the British Museum for no. 22 and the jacket illustration; the Tate Gallery for nos. 54 and 68; the Royal Archives, Windsor, for no. 85; the Public Record Office, Chancery Lane, for no. 33; the National Buildings Record R.C.H.M.E. for no. 103; Christie's for no. 3; the Trustees of the Denys Eyre Bower Bequest, Chiddingstone Castle, for nos. 12 and 13; National Power for no. 127; the Royal Institute of British Architects for no. 122; the Royal College of Physicians for no. 90; Courier Newspapers for nos. 29 and 56; British Rail for no. 4; Aerofilms Limited for no. 163; Speyhawk PLC for no. 165; Heritage Projects Limited, York for no. 168; Ted Mepham for the frontispiece and nos. 27, 143 and 153; Sabrina Izzard of Hall's Bookshop, Chapel Place for nos. 71, 79, 89, 94-96, 109 and 121; Evadna Brackett for nos. 51, 58, 61 and 92; Claude Delves for nos. 23 and 115; Keith Hetherington for no. 138; Jean Holloway for no. 119; Euan Jennings for no. 160; Brian Lazell for no. 156; and others who have generously granted permission or who, despite every effort, have not so far been traced.

Preface and Acknowledgements

I apologise to all those who will feel that I have missed out their favourite picture or part of the town or vital historical fact: unfortunately everything cannot be fitted in. I have tried to be even-handed in respect of time, place and activity. The one bias I am willing to admit is in favour of what has not been published before.

I have arranged the illustrations chronologically, but the chronology refers to the subject not the date when the picture was made. For instance, Mount Ephraim House comes in the 17th century because of royal visits in the 1660s, not because the aerial photograph was taken at that time!

An unfortunate aspect of local history writing in general has been a certain diffidence in quoting sources of information. In order to avoid the same accusation being levelled against me, I have deposited in Tunbridge Wells Reference Library a typescript of notes and references which could not be included in this volume for reasons of space, cost and lack of wide interest. I hope some will find it useful and should welcome enquiries and information.

Next, may I thank all those who have helped: Jean Mauldon and others of Tunbridge Wells Reference Library; Dr. Michael Rowlands and Dr. Ian Beavis of the Borough Museum; Kathleen Topping, Deputy Archivist, and Search Room and Photographic staff at Kent Archives Office, Maidstone; the staff at the British Library, particularly in the Map and Manuscript Rooms, and the Print Room staff at the British Museum; the National Portrait Gallery, particularly Jonathan Franklin at the Archives Office and Louisa Hearnden at the Gallery; Christie's and Sotheby's for unfailing response to queries; Christopher Chalklin for his pioneer work on the history of the town and his patient provision of information; Dr. Fred Lansberry for initiation into local history; the solicitors, Thomson, Snell and Passmore, for access to documents and for those that have been deposited with Record Offices in the past and the Buss, Merton Partnership for the documents which they deposited at Maidstone in 1984 and which have provided an invaluable source of new information – and, in hopeful anticipation, all solicitors who may be encouraged to deposit their redundant deeds with Record Offices in the future; the Camera Centre on the Pantiles for photographic service and advice; Michael Wheeler and Ron Glass for photographs and printing; John Norris of the Seeboard Milne Museum; Roger Lewis of the Tunbridge Wells Fire Brigade; Mr. Lurcook, agent of the Manor of Rusthall; Claude Delves and Kathleen Strange of those local dynasties; Mary Eldridge of the Denys Eyre Bower Bequest, Chiddingstone Castle; Sabrina Izzard of Hall's Bookshop, Chapel Place; Evadna Brackett; all householders who have answered questions and given access to deeds; and my wife for encouragement.

Finally I should like to take the opportunity to pay a belated tribute to David James Johnson, photographer and long-lived local resident and historian, who has not perhaps received the recognition he deserved for his humble but dedicated efforts to save the past before it disappeared; but some of whose contributions, pictorial and historical, may now be found in these pages.

Introduction

Tunbridge Wells is a new town. When Lord North discovered the spring in 1606, villages, farms, mansions and iron workings lay all around and had done for centuries. By chance the spot where he found the chalybeate water was in a barren area almost exactly where the counties of Kent and Sussex, the parishes of Tonbridge, Speldhurst and Frant, and the Manors of Rusthall and South Frith met. A stone in the brick paving below the sundial on the wall of the Church of King Charles the Martyr still marks the meeting of the parishes.

The town owes its shape to this coincidence. Above the spring, to the west, rose the common of Bishops Down where the freeholders of the Manor of Rusthall in Speldhurst parish had rights of grazing and where no building could take place. On the other side was the stream which marked the boundary between Kent and Sussex. Here the land was owned by Lord Abergavenny from whose seat at Eridge Lord North had been making his way towards London. The Abergavennys showed no inclination to build on their land, except in the immediate vicinity of the spring, for almost three centuries. If any building was to take place, therefore, it had to be either on the far side of the Common or in the Manor of South Frith which lay to the east of the Common in the parish of Tonbridge and stretched northwards as far as the residence of its lord at Somerhill near Tonbridge.

For a long time no permanent building took place. Lord North had the water analysed and attributed his own recovery of health to its powers. The reputation of the Wells spread and was mightily assisted by the visit of King Charles I's wife, Henrietta Maria, in 1630. She and her court were accommodated in tents on the Common but other visitors made use of what houses then existed in the neighbourhood, at Rusthall, Southborough or Tonbridge. In 1636 two little houses were put up for coffee-drinking and pipe-smoking and other conveniences of the ladies and gentlemen; and two years later a walk was formed from a grassy bank and an avenue of trees was planted, while tradesmen began to display their wares for the peripatetic water-drinkers. During the Civil War business declined but in 1663 Charles II arrived with his Queen and court.

Their Majesties are said to have stayed at Mount Ephraim House while the Court camped on the Common as before. If so, this house is the earliest of which there is any record; unless it was the cottage from which emerged the country woman who provided a wooden bowl for Lord North, became the first dipper, and lived to the fairy-tale age of 102. The monarch made merry anyhow, although the waters failed to fructify the Queen; and there were later visits when Moll Davis danced, Nell Gwyn sang and Peg Hughes softened the soldierly heart of Prince Rupert. The future King James II came and also his daughters, Mary and Anne, both to be queens. This was the time of *les eaux de scandale* which really put Tunbridge Wells on the map.

Still there was no building near the spring. The reason was that the freeholders of Rusthall Manor refused to allow lodgings which would draw business away from their houses in Rusthall and Southborough. Meanwhile, Lord Abergavenny was not interested in building on his Sussex land and the lady of South Frith had not woken up to the possibilities of this remotest corner of her manor. In 1676, however, she did make available a site for a chapel. Subscriptions were opened, and the building, the first permanent one near the spring, was completed in 1678 and named after King Charles the Martyr. The chapel became a church with a parish in 1889.

In 1680 lodging houses were built on the Culverden to the north of the Common on land belonging to Sir Charles Bickerstaffe of Wildernesse. Developments along the western border of the Common followed over the years. About the same time the Manor of Rusthall was bought by Thomas Neale who was Master of the Royal Mint. Before this the manor had been in the same ownership as South Frith. Thomas Neale it was who master-minded the development of the Pantiles. He persuaded the freeholders to accept 10 shillings per annum each as compensation for loss of grazing rights and arranged that permanent buildings should be erected, but never lodging houses. In 1682 he gave Thomas Janson, another Londoner, a 50-year lease to carry out the project. Five years after its completion most of the new buildings were burnt down; but the fire was a blessing in disguise, since the present colonnaded treasure resulted from the rebuilding.

At last the lady of South Frith, the Countess Purbeck, formerly Lady Muskerry, woke up. As her steward, Thomas Weller, was to tell the Court of Chancery in 1708, the land was 'Heathie and verry barren but the same lay in Tunbridge neare unto Tonbridge Wells very convenient to build upon'. This was the beginning of the town. The first leases were concluded in November 1684 and 33 separate transactions between then and 1696 covered an area from Mount Sion northwards as far as the Grosvenor Road and the Calverley estate.

The Manor of South Frith contained about 5,000 acres in all and was roughly triangular in shape, with its southern apex at the site of the King Charles Chapel and its eastern and western sides following the approximate lines of the Pembury Road and the road to Tonbridge through Southborough, veering towards Somerhill Park near Quarry Hill. In Tunbridge Wells the boundary follows the line of the London Road and coincides with that dividing the parishes of Tonbridge and Speldhurst. All building in the town, except that on the Pantiles and in the Culverden and Mount Ephraim areas, depended on the leasing of South Frith land and must date from after 1684.

The area of the Park and Forest of South Frith for which local men and Londoners, yeomen, tradesmen and gentlemen, must have scrambled in a gold-rush atmosphere was one of heath and woodland. The Mount Sion part was called Inhams Heath and 'Inhams Bush' was to become the Grove; further north was Calverlies Plain. The general principle of division was to allocate narrow strips fronting the planned roads for building lodging houses, with larger acreages in the 'hinterland' for the grazing of horses and livestock and the making of hay. In general the plots leased out between 1684 and 1690 have not changed to this day; they have simply been divided into smaller portions.

Within a year or two of the signing of the first leases in November 1684 the timber frames of houses began to rise, scattered over the Mount Sion hillside and up the edge of the Common and here and there to the east, to be clad with planks or hung with tiles. There was no attempt at grandeur. The houses had to be as large as possible to accommodate visitors at the peak of the season but they were built by local men using local methods, much as farmhouses were made.

In 1698 Lady Muskerry died and within a few years her son, the self-styled 'Earl of Buckingham', then approaching his majority, was faced with a crisis. Mortgages had been piling up since the time of his mother's first marriage and the mortgagees were threatening to foreclose. The young man conveyed his estates to three trustees (of whom Thomas

Weller was one) who were to manage them for the benefit of creditors, selling as much as necessary and conveying any residue back to him. By the end of 1702 most of the South Frith domains had been sold, many of the parcels being snapped up by the leaseholders. The Grove and Chapel Trust Deeds clearly formed part of the arrangements of 1702. From this date, therefore, much of the town was in the freehold ownership of a number of individuals.

A few pieces of land still belonged to the Earl of Buckingham and in 1707 he announced to Thomas Weller that he had 'bought a purchase' and wanted to mortgage his unsold lands for £600. He had made arrangements for the money from one Henry Marsh, a 'laceman' of Covent Garden. This led to a quarrel with his steward and to the Chancery suit which was discovered by Christopher Chalklin some thirty years ago. The Lord High Chancellor decided in favour of the Earl, and Thomas was obliged, in 1710, to convey the disputed site of the *Angel Inn* back to Henry Marsh as the mortgagee.

Meanwhile, Henry Marsh had been, bit by bit, giving the Earl more rope by lending further sums until the total due, with interest, amounted in 1714 to £2,102 19s. 8½d. Then he struck. But, surprise! Henry Marsh was merely acting as front man for John Brett, who had been working as agent for the Earl of Buckingham in place of old Thomas Weller. Brett was an apothecary from London who, in 1690, took over the lease of the Chapel Place block on John Wybourne's death and built the *Angel Inn*. Now, in 1715, he found himself at a stroke the master of more than one hundred acres of prime Tunbridge Wells land and houses.

He did not live long to enjoy his triumph. 'Brett Mr. John of the Wells' was buried at Tonbridge on 23 November 1719. He was married and still hoping for children but his houses and land passed to his nephew, John Brett, Doctor of Physic. The widow soon married a cleric called Pickering but the deceased had not left enough cash to pay his legacies. On the other hand, rents came rolling in and the Pickerings pocketed the proceeds. By 1727 Dr. Brett's patience was exhausted and he filed a suit; but death and delay intervened. Robert Pickering died in 1729, Dr. Brett in 1740 and Margaret in 1743. The matter was not concluded until 1752 when seven houses, including the Mount Sion Bowling Green and House, and some 50 acres of land were sold by the court for £1,670 to balance the accounts.

The 18th century was a time when Tunbridge Wells could sit back and breathe the pure air of which it boasted and enjoy itself, after the first frenzy of construction was over. The place only came to life during the season, from May to October, but there was already at the start of the century a permanent settlement of tradesmen, lodging house keepers and working people. The Presbyterians built a chapel in 1720 and this building still stands in Little Mount Sion. The chapel is notable for the ministry, from 1731 to 1752, of Thomas Bayes, father of Bayesian statistics; not to mention the sermons preached by John Wesley on several occasions between 1778 and 1784.

In 1709 the very first turnpike in Kent ran from Sevenoaks to Tunbridge Wells via Woodsgate and this remained the main route into the town from London until the road through Southborough was opened by the Maidstone and Tonbridge Turnpike Trust in 1765. It must have been via Woodsgate that Beau Nash came with his showy carriage, first to spy out the ground, then from 1735 to his death in 1761 regularly each year, though not for long. This way also came the Prince of Wales (the future George II) in 1716 and 1724 and his son Frederick, Prince of Wales but never to be king, in 1739. There were many other notable visitors: Thomas Wilson, who came in 1736, recorded the presence of seven dukes, 33 marquesses and lesser lords, 16 knights and three M.P.s, not including Prime Minister Walpole on a visit to his sick mistress.

The town had been founded on the medicinal value of the spring water. Dr. Rowzee's *Treatise* of 1632, which went to a second edition in 1671, laid down how the water was to be taken – on the spot and preferably under personal supervision! The water was reckoned to be a cure for a wide range of maladies. By this time, perhaps influenced by Queen Katharine's visits, there was particular emphasis on the water's power to cure gynaecological problems and infertility; these were eloquently dealt with in Dr. Madan's *Essay* of 1687. It was not to be expected, however, that the Merry Monarch's court would restrict itself to the pursuit of health.

Tunbridge Wells was a convenient distance from London: sufficiently remote and rural but close enough to require less than a day's travelling. Taking the waters therefore became an excuse for a holiday, and rituals based on water drinking extended to promenading, gaming and dancing. The first event of the day was a visit to the well, the ladies in *déshabille* and the gentlemen to suit. After drinking the specified dose, all returned about nine o'clock to their lodgings to dress. At ten some went to church, some to the coffee house and after prayers the company appeared on the Walks 'in greatest splendour, Music playing all the time'. They talked and walked or played at cards or dice or drank tea until it was time to return to lodgings for dinner at two. In the afternoon there were excursions or the bowling greens and on most evenings there were balls from seven to eleven. Dancing took place on the bowling green until 1739 when an Assembly Room was established on the Pantiles (on the site of the present Nos. 40-46). There was another Assembly Room on the Sussex side and rules published by Tyson, Master of Ceremonies 1780-1801, show that by this time there were two balls a week, four evenings of cards and a public tea-drinking on Sundays, and that events alternated between the two assembly rooms.

Richard Nash's civilising influence was less apparent at Tunbridge Wells than at Bath for two reasons: firstly, he had already been at Bath for 30 years before he became Master of Ceremonies at Tunbridge Wells and his ways were known (Bath's winter season did not clash with summer at the Wells); and secondly, Nash was by 1735 an older man and less demanding than in his youth. Nevertheless, he reinforced the same routine in the Kent spa. There were two main principles: firstly, that anyone in a public place could talk to anyone else, without distinction of rank or sex; and secondly, that everyone in general should do the same thing at the same time and in public.

One of the best-known Nash anecdotes concerns his insistence that gaming should be restricted to the public rooms; he was very severe on one lodging house keeper who had brought an E & O table into his house. Gambling was one of the major diversions in Tunbridge Wells, as elsewhere. Until 1738 there were no controls, but in that year Parliament prohibited the games of pharaoh, basset, hazard and ace of hearts, and in the following year that of passage. The new game of E & O (reputedly invented in Tunbridge Wells) was the gamester's retort – a sort of roulette based on Even and Odd numbers. Nash's financial arrangements with this game's promoters involved him in a scandal which soured his old age.

Little is known about his actual visits. According to Melville, he came every year before the season to supervise preparations and left after the first ball night – except in 1752 when an apoplectic fit detained him longer. However long he may have stayed, he must have laid his wig somewhere at night. Unfortunately there is no evidence where. The only first-hand witness to his presence is his signature in the King Charles vestry minutes for 1743.

When he died in Bath in 1761, his epitaph spoke of Tunbridge Wells as the 'celebrated province' which he visited every year: 'And while the necessities of State demanded his presence, He usually continued there.' With this vague summary of the Beau's visitations the town must perhaps be content. The routine which he had consolidated continued under seven more Masters of Ceremonies, but with diminishing enthusiasm, until Captain Madden resigned in 1836 and was not replaced.

The fact is that the Prince of Wales' Brighton and the seaside in general were draining away the life-blood of Tunbridge Wells as a holiday resort. Between about 1780 and 1820 a subtle change was taking place in the composition of the population and a more obvious one in the appearance of many houses. A wave of re-fronting swept over the town and many an old tile-hung or weatherboarded edifice began to boast a flat Georgian or bow-windowed Regency façade, and was christened with the name of a famous person or place. Amsinck, writing in 1810, told how General Murray had renovated his house on Mount Sion Hill, but references to other houses are lacking. Nevertheless, the physical evidence is there to behold.

At the same time a more settled population was moving in and the new residents required servants, shops and craftsmen, and somewhere to house them. The town began to extend northwards. To the east Charles Cripps built on the Windmill Fields; to the west cottages sprang up on the Crown Field, part site of the present Royal Victoria Place development; and the Hervey Town houses (and the *Bristol Arms*) were built on land belonging to the Earl of Bristol whose family name was Hervey. At the same time some of the older quarters began to fill up. Little Mount Sion, for example, one of the three 'dirty little lanes' at which Fanny Burney turned up her nose in October 1779, was developing into the street where ordinary people lived and had their shops and beer-houses. Two of the early lodging houses became over the years a continuous terrace which was known as Sion Crescent and in 1841 was home for 48 and in 1871 for 74 individuals.

On 30 December 1823 Thomas Panuwell Esquire died and in the next two or three years John Ward acquired Panuwell's 1,000-acre Calverley estate: the future *Calverley Hotel* which William Lushington had bought in 1819 and whose park he had enlarged by the purchase of adjoining fields; the Lanthorn House where the Rev. John Brett had lived; the Jack Woods quarry and spring (for the supply of stone and water) which Margaret Brett had sold to Robert Mercer in 1719; and other bits and pieces. Why John Ward should have chosen Tunbridge Wells as the place for 'banging his tremendous purse about the heads of some dozen or two of the old inhabitants, who forthwith fled and left him in full possession of their ancient abodes', as one disgruntled resident complained in the *Maidstone Journal*, is not clear – unless it was because James Burton, the father of his architect Decimus, lived at nearby Mabledon.

Building started in 1827 with the New Church (later Holy Trinity) and meanwhile work went ahead on the villas in Calverley Park, the Parade and Terrace, the Promenade (now the Crescent) and the Market Place, so that by 1835 the project was largely completed. During this time the Princess Victoria and her mother, the Duchess of Kent, came and stayed in Calverley House in 1826, 1827, 1828 and 1834, and at Boyne House on Mount Ephraim in 1835. In 1829 they stopped at the *Sussex Hotel* for a *déjeune* on the way to Buxted Park and in 1834 for a night before leaving for St Leonards in the morning.

In the year of the final royal visit Tunbridge Wells became a town. The Tunbridge Wells Improvement Act of 1835 defined the boundaries of the town and allowed it to govern itself officially. Before this, local government was loosely shared between the magistrates, the parish vestries of Tonbridge, Speldhurst and Frant, and the manorial court of Southborough which appointed its Borsholders, Ale Conners and Street Drivers and told the landlord of the *Compasses* that his sewer was overflowing and Thomas Wood to remove his dunghill from opposite the Grove Gate. In practice the same group of worthy tradesmen and gentlemen tended to shoulder the burden under whatever aegis. After 1835 all owners or occupiers of property worth £50 a year or more constituted the Improvement Commissioners and could levy a rate not exceeding 2 shillings in the pound.

The need for public services was becoming apparent. Until the 19th century it had been a private world. You had your well for water or shared it with neighbours; you paid for emptying the 'house of office' from time to time; you paid also for the 'watch' and the 'highways'; and you had to pay rates, like it or not, for the undeserving poor. However, in 1801 the population was only an estimated 1,000; by 1841 it had increased to 8,302. In 1814 the plumber, Thomas Taylor, piped water to The Pantiles and Mount Sion areas from the Tangier spring and in 1826 was bought out by the Tunbridge Wells Water Company. Similarly, John Ward provided a mains supply to his new estate from the Jack Woods spring. In 1834 a gas company was formed and the streets were lit by gas within two years. A start was made on a sewage system; a 'scavenger' was appointed; and, finally, the town acquired its own little police force under the 'vigilant' Superintendent Thompson.

Then the railway arrived. On 19 September 1845 a ceremonial train steamed into the Jack Woods Station (the old goods station) in Tunbridge Wells. A tunnel under Mount Pleasant opened up the Central Station in 1846 on the site of the Mount Pleasant Brewery, and a further tunnel under the Grove gave Aretas Akers the chance to sell his Belle Vue house which stood above the southern exit, together with the land below, so that the railway could push on to Hastings. On 23 June 1849 the Queen and Prince Albert tested the route on an apparently unpremeditated visit to the Queen Dowager at the *Calverley Hotel*.

The other line, belonging to the London, Brighton and South Coast Railway, terminated at the West Station from 1866 until 1872, when a loop was built connecting the two systems through the fields at the back of Mount Sion. The population of the town reached 10,000 in 1851 and 24,000 by 1881. Development of the Calverley acres, mainly by the builder William Willicombe, continued to the east and north and up the Pembury Road; Camden Park followed; and Lord Abergavenny built in Nevill and Hungershall Parks and on Broadwater Down. Meanwhile, less select development started in the St John's Road area and elsewhere, and a general filling-in of empty spaces continued.

With the houses came the churches and with the churches very often the schools. Holy Trinity had taken on the parochial district of Tunbridge Wells in 1833, severing the historic connection with Tonbridge; Christ Church, opening in 1840, acquired a district in 1856; St John's (1858), St James' (1862), St Mark's (1866), St Peter's (1875) and St Barnabas' (1881) followed; and finally a funny little parish was created in 1889, in response to a retiring plea from the Rev. Pope, for the oldest church in the town. The Nonconformists, starting with the Mount Sion Presbyterians in 1720, multiplied in their turn, but the old chapel fell into disrepair, was rescued briefly by the Congregationalists in 1830, only to be sold into secular use in 1875. The Congregational church of 1847 on Mount Pleasant was aggrandised with its temple-like portico in 1866. In 1838, meanwhile, the Roman Catholics built St Augustine's in Grosvenor Road.

Most of these churches had their schools for the poorer classes, 'National' for the Anglicans and 'British' for the Nonconformists. The girls of King Charles the Martyr moved in 1813 to a separate establishment on the corner of Little Mount Sion and

Warwick Road until the Rev. Pope bought Murray House for them in 1858, when their old premises were taken over by the Christ Church boys. Princess Victoria opened the National School off the Camden Road which bore her name until sold in 1961. Until 1875 a 'British' school for the daughters of Nonconformist parents occupied a schoolroom adjoining the chapel on Little Mount Sion. Private schools of varying sizes and degrees of professionalism, offering a more genteel education, waxed and waned continually. One of the earliest was Fry's Sion Crescent Academy for young gentlemen on Little Mount Sion, from about 1800 to 1830; Fry was surely the schoolmaster of that name called on by the future Duchess of Wellington to help her son in 1812. In 1887 came the first recognisable part of the present-day school scene with the opening of the Skinners' School on the St John's Road. The Girls' Grammar School followed, starting in the London Road in 1905 and moving to Southfield by 1912.

In 1855 the first real Tunbridge Wells newspaper began publication. The man behind the *Tunbridge Wells Gazette* was John Colbran, already known for his *Guide* of 1840. Amongst matters reported by the *Gazette* in the next few years were a change in the local electoral system and the 'Webber Riots'. By 1860 the number of £50 householders eligible to be Commissioners had increased to several hundred but meetings were sparsely attended and it was decided to adopt a system made possible by the Local Government Act of 1858. There were to be 24 Commissioners, one-third elected annually by the votes of all owners or occupiers of property worth £30 a year or more. The wealthier men got more votes, up to six for property valued at £250 or over. This system was initiated in September 1860. Three months earlier Dr. William Webber had arrived.

Dr. Webber was the Mr. Grouser of Tunbridge Wells. Towards the beginning of the 1864 summer season Edwards the butcher, on the London Road at the bottom of Mount Sion, was employing Willicombe the builder to excavate a cellar in front of his shop. They came across the remains of a drain. It was bricked up at each end and appeared dry and inoffensive but Dr. Webber happened to pass by. He complained to Mr. Wright, the Town Surveyor, and to the police. Not satisfied, he wrote to Sir George Grey at the Home Office, and Dr. Hunter was sent down on the next train. He found nothing wrong. The local doctors censured their colleague but the townsfolk, particularly the lodging house keepers who saw their visitors being scared away, were not content. On 2 July one thousand, some say two thousand, men and youths crowded the bottom of Mount Sion outside Webber's house. Stones were thrown, windows were broken, the effigy of a pig was burned, and the balcony of the house was set on fire. Rain came and saved further damage – but not Dr. Webber. By August Dr. Webber was gone, saying in a parting letter to the *Gazette* that his only regret on leaving the town was that he had ever entered it.

From 1862 to 1878 the town was presided over by the Hon. F. G. Molyneux who rebuilt Earl's Court on Mount Ephraim for himself. Then an agitation commenced to do away with the plural voting system of 1860. At length it succeeded and a special train delivered the town's charter on 27 February 1889. There were to be four wards, north, south, east and west, which would each elect six councillors for three years. All ratepayers, numbering 4,500 initially, could vote by secret ballot. John Stone-Wigg, Chairman of the old Commissioners, became the first Mayor and W. C. Cripps, grandson of the Windmill Fields builder, began a long and distinguished career as Town Clerk. Arms were granted with the motto 'Do well, doubt not'.

The population increased from over 24,000 in 1881 to 33,373 in 1901 and house-building continued apace. In 1870 the Great Hall was built to complement the waning Assembly Room on the Pantiles as a venue for public functions. In 1876 the Queen came to Tunbridge Wells for the last time; but only to spend Boxing Day with her daughter at Dornden on the Langton Road. In 1878 the old *Kentish Royal Hotel* was demolished and replaced by the *Grand*, now the Kentish Mansions. Two years later the equally venerable *Sussex Hotel* on the Lower Walk ended its days as a hotel, and the house where Princess Victoria had watched a review of the Yeomanry in 1834 opened as the Bishops Down Spa.

In 1894 Sir David Salomons Bart. became Mayor and under his influence the town borrowed money and built a power station near the Grosvenor Bridge, supplied the central area of the town with electricity and made a profit. The first year of the new century saw Tunbridge Wells distinguish itself with the pioneer municipal telephone system in England. Within two years, however, this was in private hands and two enterprising decades were crowned in 1909 by the grant from King Edward VII of the title 'Royal Tunbridge Wells', in recognition of historic connections.

In 1900 the Eye and Ear Hospital moved from the old *Sussex Hotel* building on the Pantiles to Fairlawn House, Mount Sion, and Percy Adams' new building for the General Hospital, in tardy celebration of the Queen's Jubilee, was opened in 1904. The town had never been short of doctors but the hospital began life as the Dispensary in the High Street in 1829. It moved to the Grosvenor Road in 1842 and was gradually enlarged to meet needs. In 1878 the Eye and Ear Dispensary opened in Vale Road and moved to the Pantiles ten years later. Both hospitals, General and Eye and Ear, amalgamated in the present Kent and Sussex buildings in 1934.

The 1914-18 war caused the loss of 776 local lives and a harmless hole in the Calverley grounds from an errant Zeppelin bomb. Between the wars the population remained static but 713 council houses were built, starting with an estate at Rusthall in 1926. Generally the appearance of the town changed little. In 1934 the county boundary was moved to include Broadwater Down, the Ramslye council estate and the Hawkenbury cemetery; and the Council decided to build itself a new Town Hall.

Since 1858 the Town Hall had been Decimus Burton's unsuccessful Market Place in the Calverley Road. Now a public competition was held for a new Civic Centre. The prize-winning design is there for all to see, where John Brett's Lanthorn House and then Burton's Parade and Terrace once proudly stood. The building was brought into use by stages, starting in the first year of the Second World War.

Active service deaths this time, at 166, were far fewer than during the first war but death, damage and disturbance at home were more severe. A total of 741 bombs in 1940 and a few flying bombs in 1944 caused 15 deaths and 70 serious injuries, together with the destruction of 13 houses and severe damage to another ninety-eight. The Calverley grounds were again a random target but this time the bandstand pavilion succumbed to incendiary bombs. No. 10 Broadwater Down became General Montgomery's headquarters and was visited by the King; Bredbury, built between 1850 and 1865 on Mount Ephraim, became the regional headquarters for the South-East; Pembury Hospital took in much of Guy's Hospital; and the Skinners' School played host to Colfe's Grammar School. Tunbridge Wells received some 5,000 evacuees over the course of three days.

If the inter-war period was somewhat static, the post-war one has been hectic. The 1944 Act changed the face of schooling in the town. New secondary modern schools came into being at Huntley's and Sandown Court, and a Technical High School opposite the *Cross Keys*, while older establishments like Skinners' and the Girls' Grammar were slotted into the tri-partite system as grammar schools or as secondary modern schools like Bennett Memorial, and new primary schools mushroomed. Privatisation followed nationalisation in the public utilities; but, in the sphere of health, the Kent and Sussex and Pembury Hospitals continue to serve, complemented by the new Nuffield. The Planning Acts of 1947 have had their impact on the physical appearance of the town in the second half of the 20th century.

The planning scene can be divided into 'losses and replacements'; 'new buildings'; and 'rescues and adaptations'. Examples of losses include the Pump Room on the Pantiles replaced by the Union Square shops and offices; the Old Town Hall replaced by offices and Sainsbury's; St Augustine's Roman Catholic Church replaced by Tesco; early 19th-century houses in Church Road replaced by office blocks; old cottages in Warwick Road and Little Mount Sion replaced by untidy car parks; the 1904 hospital wing replaced by the new Meadow Road multi-storey car park; the Monson Road baths replaced by new Town Hall offices; finally and almost fatally to the integrity of the Mount Sion scene, Eden and Murray Houses replaced by town house terraces, and Walmer House replaced by a shop and office block.

Among the new buildings are the Hawkenbury Land Registry; the multi-storey car park and the health insurance offices in Crescent Road; the St John's Road Swimming and Sports Centre; the nice new Mazda offices on Mount Ephraim; the red fortress of Safeway by the Central Station; and all those sheds on the Industrial Estate. Among the rescues are, first and foremost, Holy Trinity Church, transformed into an Arts Centre; the Mount Pleasant Church, converted into a Habitat store; the Great Hall shopping arcade and offices with, at the rear, the most beautiful car park in the kingdom; the Little Mount Sion chapel, radiantly refurbished as a type-setting office; several Burton buildings in Calverley Road and Garden Street; and, last but not least, on the Pantiles, the Dust's renovation and the latest chapter in the saga of the *Sussex Hotel* and Sarah Baker's theatre.

At Calverley Road a timid step has been made in the direction of pedestrianisation. In the High Street, Christ Church is to be demolished in favour of a combination of church, community centre and shopping mall; on the Pantiles a Heritage Exhibition is housed in the old Assembly Rooms; the blighted back of the Calverley precinct is now in thrall to crane and dozer but will arise shining in a year or two as the Royal Victoria Place shopping mall; and at the southern end of the town the West Station has become a restaurant adjoining a new Sainsbury's supermarket and D.I.Y. store. The line was closed in 1985 but there are plans for a private railway to use it. The main line to Hastings was at last electrified in 1986 after 30 years of grunting diesels had succeeded the puffing locomotives of yore.

In 1974 the borough ceased to exist and became a 'District' embracing Speldhurst in one direction and Benenden in the other, but not Tonbridge. Mr. Girling retired as third and last Town Clerk and now a Chief Executive reigns supreme. The problems which face the town presently are those of traffic and parking and of changes in the pattern of shopping and pressures for office space and housing. The population was 38,397 in 1951 and had reached an estimated 45,000 (on the old Borough basis) by 1988. Much was achieved by Council housing before the right to buy put a stop to it; but new private venture estates have multiplied and in-filling and sub-division of larger houses have increased the number of dwellings without making any impact on the rise in house prices, which would have made clever old John Brett a multi-millionaire in return for his foreclosure on the Earl of Buckingham. No doubt they would both hope that the town continues to do well; and no doubt it will if it does not burst at the seams first.

Tents on the Common: 1596~1676

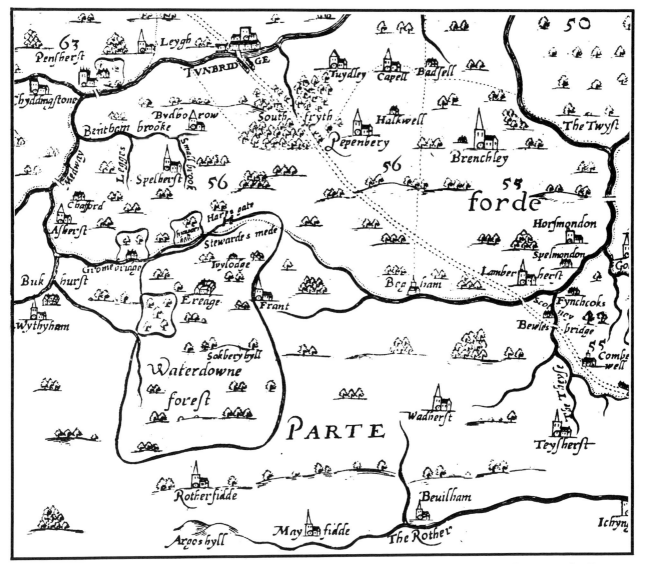

1. Symonson's map of Kent published in 1596, just 10 years before the discovery of the Wells, shows Bydborow, Spelherst, Ereage, Frant and the road to Rye going through the South fryth wood; but the nearest to the future Tunbridge Wells are Haresgate, Hungershall and the river Grom running through Gromebridge to join the Medway and dividing Kent from Sussex.

2. Frances, daughter of Sir Francis Walsingham, belongs to the story of Tunbridge Wells because Queen Elizabeth gave her the Manor of South Frith after her second husband, the Earl of Essex, was beheaded in 1601. Her first husband was Sir Philip Sidney (of Penshurst, the poet) and her third was the Earl of Clanricarde who built Somerhill House (see plate 16).

3. Dudley, 3rd Lord North (1581-1666), was only 25 years old when he discovered the chalybeate spring, but seems to have been suffering from the entertainment given by James I to his brother-in-law King Christian of Denmark at a time when diplomacy demanded the ability to drink the guests under the table – and the Danes did not go under easily.

4.   Lord North discovers the spring in 1606. In the absence of a photographer on the scene, what better substitute than British Rail's imaginative mural painted in 1989 on the Central Station wall! The girl with the beaker is Mrs. Humphreys, who is said to have become the first 'dipper' and to have died a centenarian.

5.   The spring is only 50 yards from this stone which marks the meeting point of parishes and counties.

chiefest Chymists of this age, doubted whether he should call the Empsenses *Aqua Alumirom* or *Nitrous*, so harda thing it is exactly to distinguish in things, that are compounded and permixt. But it is now time we should go to *Tunbridge* Water.

CHAPTER VI.

Of Tunbridge *Water.*

THe Water commonly known here amongst us by the name of *Tunbridge* Water, are two small Springs contiguous together, about some four miles Southward from the town of *Tunbridg* in *Kent*, from which they have their name, as being the nearest Towne in *Kent* to them. They are seated in a valley compassed about with stony hills, so barren, that there groweth no-

thing but heath upon the same. Just there doe *Kent* and *Sussex* meete, and one may with less than half a breath run from those Springs into *Sussex*.

It pleased our gracious Queene *Marie* to grace this Water by her presence two years agoe, so that those Springs may justly be called, as some do call them now, *Queene Maries Wells*. The taste of the water is not unpleasant to those, who have a while been used to it, and it is a sure thing, that no man is able to drink half so much of any other liquor, though never so pleasant unto him, as he may of this. What other minerals it runneth through, besides Iron and the *rubrick* of Iron, which is seen on the ground, over which the water runneth, is not yet well known, for there hath been as yet no digging near about the same. The greater part of those that drink of it, are purged by stoole

6.   Contemporary testimony to the barrenness of the surrounding country is contained in this extract from *The Queen's Wells* published by Dr. Lodwick Rowzee of Ashford in 1632, two years after the visit of Queen Henrietta Maria. He also comments on the close proximity of Sussex, but fails to mention the need to jump the stream forming the border!

7.   Extracts from an instruction dated 10 June 1665 to the masters of the royal 'Tents, Toils and Pavilions' about the pitching of tents in 1665 and 1666. This shows that the Queen's 'Pavilion Royal' was to be pitched at Tunbridge (Tunbridge Wells Common?) in 1666. Other manuscripts reveal that tents were commonly used for royal excursions.

8. Mount Ephraim House is on the left of the row and behind it is the old Chancellor House, demolished about 1930, and named after Judge Jeffreys. Next to Mount Ephraim House is the Chalet (see plate 108) and the large building is the *Wellington Hotel* built in about 1875. In the foreground is the boundary of the Upper Cricket Ground (see plate 156) and, on the right, the Wellington Rocks. Was it hereabouts that the Court camped while the King and Queen stayed in Mount Ephraim House?

9. Colbran's 1840 *Guide* mentions a common alternative belief that the Court camped in Southborough. The suggestion is given some plausibility by this newly-discovered British Museum manuscript which shows that the Queen had a tent at 'Bownes' in 1663: and where could 'Bownes' be if not 'Bounds'? If so, did the King and Queen stay in Great Bounds House?

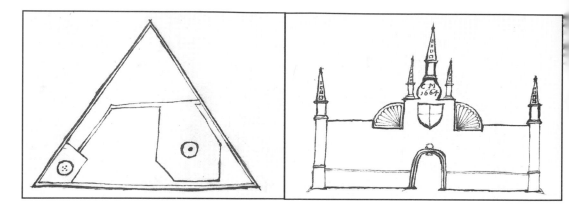

10. Dr. Edward Browne travelled widely in England and Europe in the 17th century and sketched what he saw. Thanks to his celebrated father, author of *Religio Medici*, his drawings are preserved in the British Museum. This is not one of his best but is a rare contemporary view. The initials stand for Charles Muskerry, who refurbished the well in 1664.

11. This anonymous engraving provides another view of Lord Muskerry's well in 1664, with the stone wall (looking rather thin perhaps?) that replaced Lord Abergavenny's wooden rails and a dipper's hand proffering a beaker of the precious fluid. Music was evidently important. The position and permanency of the temple structure are matters for speculation; the sense of rusticity is not.

12. Charles I (*left*) by Matthew Snelling and his son, Charles II (*above*), drawn from life by Samuel Cooper, form an interesting comparison in the Stuart Room at Chiddingstone Castle. Both have their place in Tunbridge Wells history, the chapel being named (for reasons never precisely stated) after the former, and the latter, with his court, having done much to popularise the Wells.

13. Nell Gwyn also played her part in advertising the charms of the place: she was probably there in 1666 and perhaps in 1668 and 1669. Lely's splendid painting of her and her son by the King now hangs above the two Kings' miniatures at Chiddingstone. The Streatfeilds of Chiddingstone comprised a pocket of Royalist support in mainly Parliamentary Kent.

15. Unfortunately, no portraits seem to exist of Lady Muskerry or her first two husbands: Lord Muskerry, who was killed in the sea battle with the Dutch in 1665; and Robert Purbeck, who died abroad in a duel in 1686. We must therefore be content with a portrait of her third and worst, the gambler and rake, Robert 'Beau' Fielding (1651-1712).

14. Ulick de Burgh (1604-57) son of Frances and the Earl of Clanricarde, became the first Marquess of Clanricarde and inherited Somerhill and the South Frith Manor. While he was commanding Royalist forces in Ireland during the Commonwealth, his daughter Margaret and her mother were in exile in Paris. It was there that Margaret met her future husband, Lord Muskerry.

16. Somerhill House was built about 1610-20, 'at a very large expense on a pleasant eminence', by the Earl of Clanricarde. This early print is almost identical to one dated 1783. The house was one of the nearest mansions to the Wells in the early days and seems to have served as an aristocratic lodging house during the 'season'.

17. This vignette from Colbran's 1843 *Guide* claimed to depict from life the 1636 Coffee House or Pipe Office in Pink Alley, demolished in 1842. One place or the other was said to have been the residence of Mrs. Humphreys, the first dipper, but was not necessarily, of course, the cottage from which she magically emerged to serve Lord North.

18. A painted legend on this shop, No. 7 The Pantiles, now The Vintry, claims that it was built as a private house in 1660 and converted into a shop in 1768; but the only evidence seems to be that it has always been painted thus. This photograph of Durrant's Wineshop and staff shows how little has changed since 1887, Queen Victoria's jubilee year.

19. Nos. 12-16 The Pantiles. The plaque on the balcony states 1664, but on what authority is unclear. There is some evidence from manor records that Richard Constable was allowed a shop on the Walks as early as 1671, on payment of 4d. to each freehold tenant. His shop may have been in this location – but would it not have been burnt down in the fire of 1687?

The First Buildings: 1678~1718

20. The Chapel of King Charles the Martyr was almost certainly the first substantial building in Tunbridge Wells. Built by public subscription to fill the visitors' need for a place of worship, it was opened in 1678 and doubled in size in 1690. Early illustrations, except the view on Kip's engraving showing the original side entrance (see plate 36), are lacking. This photograph shows the old gallery entrance on the other side.

21. The glory of the chapel, its plaster ceiling, was the work of Henry Doogood, chief plasterer to Sir Christopher Wren, and a local man, John Wetherell. Local men also did the building work. David Johnson (see plate 148) took this photograph about 1930.

22. Thomas Neale Armiger (i.e. Esquire), creator of the Pantiles, bought the Manor of Rusthall from Lady Muskerry in about 1680 and persuaded the freehold tenants to allow development. He was Master of the Mint from about 1678 until his death in 1699.

23. The *Angel Inn* was one of the first buildings on South Frith land about 1690. This original drawing by Emma Marshall for her 1902 book *Up and Down the Pantiles* nevertheless looks quite accurate, showing the inn sign over the road (as in Kip's engraving), the flat-fronted *Angel Inn* and the fences round the chapel and the spring.

24. Burlington House was a good example of an early Tunbridge Wells lodging house. Built by Nicholas Wood, fellmonger, in about 1689, it never left the family ownership until demolished about 1880. This drawing, from the *Belle Vue Magazine* (see plate 100), is by one of the Akers children. Jane Akers, their grandmother, was living here when she died in 1842.

25. This charming picture from the sketch book of a visitor in 1824 shows the house now known as Thackeray's on account of the novelist's sojourn there in 1860. It was previously called Rock Villa. Another old-style house, it has been dated to the 1660s but, being on South Frith land in Tonbridge parish, is unlikely to have been built before 1684.

26.   Edward Martin was one of the carpenters who built the chapel. In 1684 he leased a strip of Mount Sion from Lady Muskerry and built two lodging houses known as Martins Upper and Lower Houses. The Upper House has gone, but the tile-hanging shown in this photograph reveals the Lower House still lurking behind a High Street shop-front.

27.   Behind the tree is another early lodging house (No. 69 London Road) which has retained its original appearance. Ashton Lodge (as it was later known) appears on Bowra's map as John Jeffery's and remained in this family until a later John went bankrupt in 1816. On the street corner at the right is Jordan House, 19th-century home of Tunbridge Ware and the Burrows family. This photograph was taken in 1934.

28. The Middle Grove House, just below the Grove, was another of the original lodging houses. It became a school in 1845 and was demolished to make way for Christchurch and Grove Avenues in about 1900.

29. The Manor House on Bishops Down might be expected to be as ancient as Rusthall Manor itself, but this house was used as a lodging house rather than a manor house, and probably dates from the same late 17th-century era as other lodging houses.

VD? DEAD or self aborted Babies ? No contraception

30. Poor Queen Anne had umpteen babies but the Duke of Gloucester was the only one to survive, and even he died at the age of eleven. This portrait, after Godfrey Kneller, was painted *c*.1694. In 1698 he fell while playing soldiers on the Walks and his mother gave £100 to have the area paved. No paving had been laid when she came next and, irate, Anne never set foot in the town again.

31a. & b. When Anne's instructions were eventually obeyed, pantiles were used for paving. These are a few of the originals that remain. Pans (as in 'saucepan') were anciently made of hard baked clay and the same material came to be used for square floor tiles. Pantiles were then used for paving and, later, for roofing.

THE PANTILES
ALONG THE FOOT OF THESE STEPS ARE ALL THAT REMAIN OF THE SQUARE TILES WITH WHICH THE UPPER WALK WAS ORIGINALLY PAVED IN 1700. AT THE EXPENSE OF PRINCESS ANNE, AFTERWARDS QUEEN ANNE.

32. Two lodging houses, built by Philip Seale in 1689 and 1694, were the origins of the row of tile-hung, weather-boarded houses pictured in this Camburn postcard. The terrace was later known as Sion Crescent and Queen Anne's Mansion. See also plate 141.

Old Tunbridge Wells. Little Mt. Sion. Queen Anne stayed at House with Porch.

33.   Much of the early history of the Tonbridge parish area of the town is derived from this manuscript which records the action brought by the Earl of Buckingham against his steward, Thomas Weller, in 1708. The sides of the document have had to be omitted but certain names of places (Bowling Green, Chapel, Common) and people (Lord Abergavenny, Thomas Weller, John Brett) can be discerned.

34. Built in 1699 by Thomas Ashenhurst, this is probably the lodging house to which Thomas Wilson referred in 1736: '... Woods and Brothers upon the top of Mount Sion near the Bowling Green. A very handsome house.' The house accounts for 1704-08, preserved in a Chancery case, reveal that Sir Samuel and his brother Francis Dashwood were visitors in 1704 and 1706. The Dashwoods were Lords of Rusthall Manor after Thomas Neale.

Thomas Wilson ↑ 1734

35. 'Ashenhurst's Great House' (see above) looks like a brick-built Queen Anne house, but when the owner came to make renovations in 1989 he found timber-framing. The house was bought by Nicholas Wood and remained in his family until 1831. Between 1780 and 1786 it was divided into two and later changed its name to Berkeley Place.

From Kip to Bowra: 1719-38

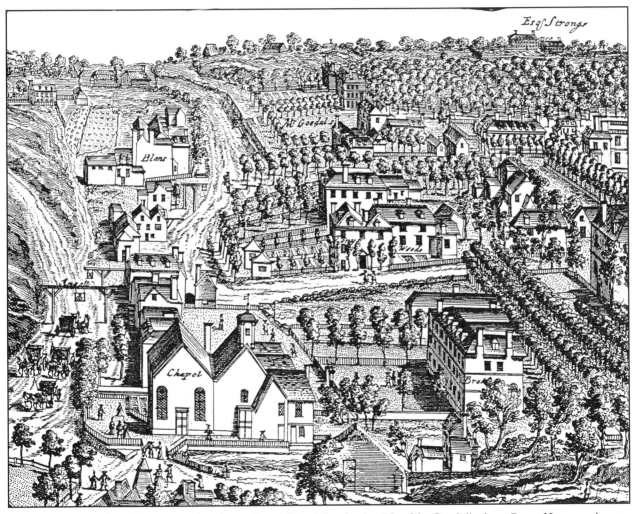

36.   This detail from Kip's engraving shows, from left to right: the *Angel Inn*; Mr. Goodal's three Grove Houses; a house marked 'Tovy', later called Bolton House, then Stone Court, and demolished about 1849; 'Woods' which ought to be Sion House but looks wrong; Brett's boarding house (Chapel House); the Grove; and on the horizon Esq. Strong's, the original *Calverley Hotel* building.

37. Kip's engraving of a drawing made by Badeslade for Harris's *History of Kent* in 1718 or 1719 is the earliest illustration of the Walks. Compare the view of the well itself with Dr. Browne's sketch (see plate 10). Land to the right of the *Gloucester Tavern* (now Strawsons) and Mr. Hunt's (*Duke of York*) belonged to Lord Abergavenny.

38. James II's likeness to Thomas Neale (see plate 22) was remarked upon but was apparently coincidental. As Duke of York, he came to the Wells several times between 1670 and 1687, helping to popularise the High Rocks and hoping that the waters would assist two successive wives to produce an heir. His daughters, Mary and Anne, both queens later, came too.

39. The Duke of Marlborough's sister, Arabella Churchill, became the mistress of James II (then Duke of York), following, it is said, a lucky fall from her horse and display of underskirt in his company. She later married Colonel Godfrey and, as Mrs. Godfrey, enters the history of Tunbridge Wells as guardian of George Anne Bellamy's mother (see plate 40). This portrait is by Sir Peter Lely.

40. According to her autobiography, the actress George Anne Bellamy's grandfather was a rich hop-planter called Seal who bought an estate on Mount Sion. His widow ran a lodging house there and was befriended by Mrs. Godfrey. In financial difficulties, she let Mrs. Godfrey look after her daughter, who, at school in London, was seduced by Lord Tyrawley (seen here on the right).

41. The product of this seduction was George Anne Bellamy, who became a celebrated actress and is here pictured on stage with the great David Garrick. The family connection with Mount Sion rests entirely on her autobiography. A 'Seale' did own houses on Little Mount Sion but he was a plumber and an Anglican; the hop-planter was supposedly a Quaker who gave land for the Presbyterian chapel.

42. According to one story, a Baptist named Jordan obtained land for the Presbyterian chapel from the Quaker Seal; but documentary evidence suggests it was the plumber, Philip Seale, who owned the land. The chapel was opened in 1720. This photograph was given to the Museum by the great-granddaughter of William Johnston, who was minister after Bayes, the statistician, from 1752 to 1776. It shows, below the chapel, the *Jolly Sailor* and the Montgomery cottages, now demolished.

43. The origin of the names Mount Sion and Mount Ephraim is problematic. According to one story, Cromwellian troops were stationed on these hills during the Civil War, and their Puritan beliefs suggested the biblical names; but another story implicates the whimsical landlord of a tavern who put up a sign saying 'Mount Sion'. He is named by Sprange as 'Jordan' and by Benge Burr as 'Mathews' – and the *Grove Tavern*'s first two landlords were so named! Johnson's photograph dates probably from the 1920s.

A trew and parfit Inventtory of the
goods and Chattles of Thomas mathews
~~dec[...]~~ late deceased of the
Parrish of tunbridge on mount sion
at tunbridgewells in Kent taken and
Aprised this 30 Day of October 1718
by us whose names hear under sett
as followeth ——

Imprimes = ~~in the kitten~~   l - s - d

his waveing Apparrell and
his money in his purse ——} 3 - 0 - 0

in the kitten one Clock one Iack
2 = Spitts 1 - Dripping pan fire shovell
tongs an Irons and hollows
12 Dishes of putter 2 - Dusen
of plate randle thitch thay out
A table and other small things } 3 - 2 - 6

in the pallor - 3 - tabls - 9 - thay out — 0 - 15 - 0

in the pallor Chamber one bed
and all belonging to it one
Case of Drawers - 2 - tabls
3 - thay out and other small
things } 3 - 0 - 0

in the kitten Chamber one bed
and all belonging to it one
table - 4 - thay out } 2 - 10 - 0

in the garrott - 3 - beds - 2 - tabls
4 - thay out - 2 - Chests - 2 - boxes } 3 - 2 - 0

linen - 8 - payer of sheet - 6 - table
cloths napking and towells } 2 - 10 - 0

in the seller beer and some other
lumber } 1 - 5 - 0

in the wash house - 2 - tobs - 2 - bellows 0 - 5 - 0

without Dores - 2 - pigs — 0 - 18 - 0

for things fob got and
unseen and old lumber } 0 - 5 - 0

                                          19 - 12 - 6

the ⌐mark⌐
of wm⌐ Baines
Philip Seale

44. The *Compasses*, probably built about 1700, consisted originally of the rear portion of the present building. The Probate Inventory, reproduced here, of landlord Thomas Mathews (it was 'John' Mathews at the *Grove Tavern*) who died in 1718 shows that there were a kitchen and parlour on the ground floor, two bedrooms on the first floor and an attic above.

45. (*Facing page*) Much information on house occupancy can be extracted from the Poor Rate books of Tonbridge parish; the difficulty is that houses are not named or numbered but identified by the occupant's name. This example from 1728 lists Lord Percival (*Calverley Hotel*); Mr. Goodal (*Grove Houses*); William Wood (*Burlington House*); Alexander Ashdown (*Murray House*); and Philip Seale (*Little Mount Sion*) among others.

and for a field and 3 Houses	05:	00:	00
Mr Chapman for Hills	00:	12:	00
Mathew Calverly	00:	16:	00
Mr Forrard	00:	12:	00
Thomas Moyse	00:	12:	00
Lord Percivale	01:	12:	00
Will:m Wood	02:	00:	00
and for the little house or Occup:	00:	04:	00
Alexander Ashdowne	00:	08:	00
Mr Philip Seale	00:	12:	00
for Constables fields	00:	06:	00
for Harrisons field and one other field	00:	08:	00
Will:m Fry for a New house	00:	10:	00
Mrs Walton for Mr Hoopers	01:	12:	00
John Mathews	00:	04:	00
Tho: Seale	00:	08:	00
Mr Beadle for Simon Linchs	01:	00:	00
Mr Betts or Occup: of a New house & bowling Greene	01:	14:	00
Mr Walton	02:	00:	00
Widd: Scoones	01:	00:	00
Mr Bland for Riders	01:	08:	00
Widd: Mathews	00:	12:	00
Tho: Banns	01:	00:	00
Mr Pickerring for the Angell or Occup:	03:	00:	00
for the Hand & Sheares or Occup:	00:	16:	00
Sarah Randell for Brick lands	00:	14:	00
Nicholas Wood for Drueth	00:	08:	00

46.   The original *Calverley Hotel* house was almost certainly built by William Strong (see plate 36) around 1700 and bought from his heirs by Lord Percival, seen here with his wife. He became M.P. for Harwich in 1727 and was active in promoting the Georgia settlement. In 1734, as his diary records on 26 March, he gave 'Mount Pleasant at Tunbridge Wells', a house in London and the *George Inn*, on Snow Hill in London, with a total rental value of £319 a year, to his son to enable him to stand for Parliament.

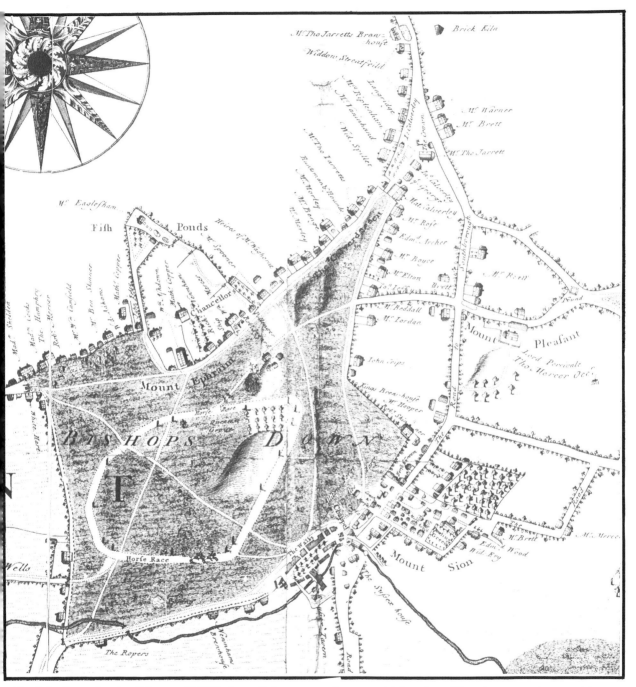

47. John Bowra's splendid map of 1738 helps to link ratepayers' names with locations. There is a general map, with separate plans of the Pantiles and Mount Sion. Here we see most of the town on the general map, showing many houses which still exist, altered perhaps, up the London road and along Mount Ephraim, with the names of their owners.

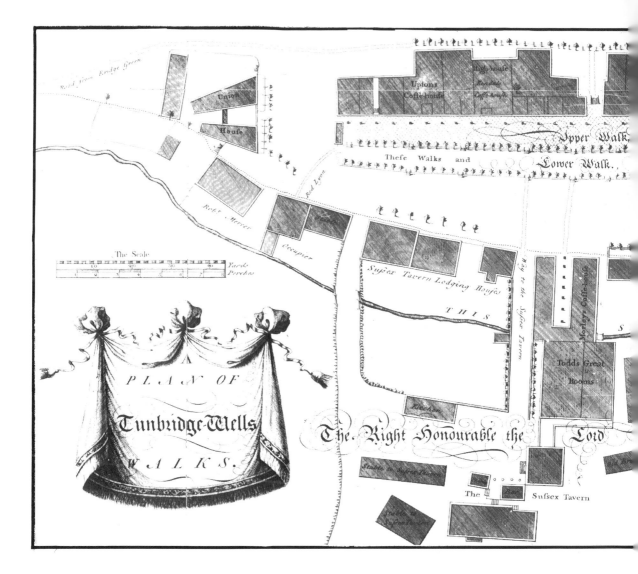

48. Bowra's map was occasioned by the dispute between the Lord of the Manor and his freehold tenants which culminated in the Rusthall Manor Act of 1739. The solution was a lottery. The freeholders drew Lot B, leaving A and C to the lord. Lot B, known as the Walks Estate, ran from the Great Gaming Room to the Flat House.

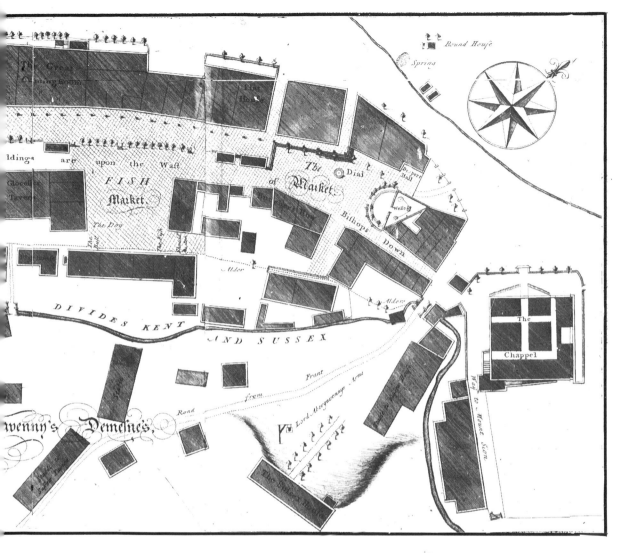

The Great
Cloathing Room

The House

Idings are upon the Waft

FISH

Gloceter
Tavern

Market

The Dog

The Bull

The Fish

Alder

DIVIDES KENT

AND SUSSEX

The Dial
of Market

Bishops Down

Upper
Mall

Wells

Alder

Alder

Round Houfe

Spring

The
Chappel

Way to Mount Sion

venny's Demesnes,

Road

from

Frant

Yᵉ Lord Abergavenny Arms

The

To the Right Honourable
William Lord Abergavenny,
THIS SURVEY OF
Tunbridge Wells,
Is Moft Humbly Dedicated,
By HIS LORDSHIP'S
Moft Obedient Servant
John Bowra.

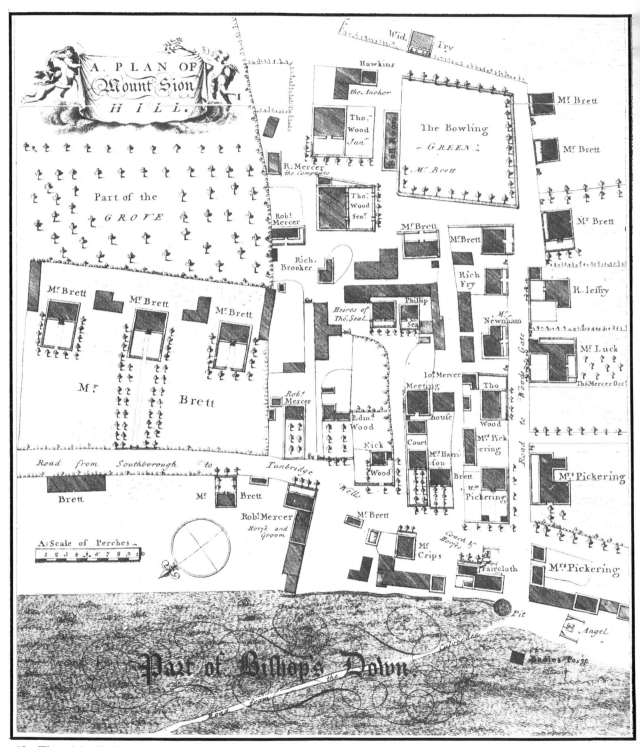

49. The original building plots, going up from the High Street and sideways from Mount Sion Road, can be distinguished in Bowra's plan of Mount Sion. Note the strip, including the *Compasses*, owned by Robert Mercer and the amount owned by Mr. Brett (the Grove Houses and the Bowling Green block) and by his widow, Mrs. Pickering (the Chapel Place block).

Heyday of the Masters
of Ceremonies: 1739-1800

50. Richard 'Beau' Nash, Master of Ceremonies at Bath since 1705, established himself in the same role in Tunbridge Wells in 1735. He came with a flourish each year and stayed a short while. This portrait used to hang in the former Great Gaming Room; Nash the Postmaster, a reputed relative, is said to have given it to the Town Hall.

The remarkable characters who were at Tunbridge Wells with Richardson in 1748 from a drawing in his possession with reference in his own writing

1748 Aug:
1 Dr. Johnson
2 Bp. of Salisbury (Dr Gilbert)
3 Ld. Harcourt

4 Mr. Cibber (Colley)
5 Mr. Garrick
6 Mrs Frasi (The Singer)
7 Mr Nash

8 Miss Chudleigh (Dutch of Kingston)
9 Mr Pitt (Earl of Chatham)
10 A. Onslow (The Speaker)
11 Ld. Powis

12 Dutch of Norfolk
13 Miss Banks
14 Lady Lincoln
15 Mr Lyttelton (Lord Lyttelton) Afterwards

16 The Baron (A German Gamester)
17 Anonym (Mr Richardson)
18 Mrs Onslow

19 Miss Onslow
20 Mrs Johnson (The Dr's Wife)
21 Mr Whiston
22 Loggan the Artist
23 The Woman of the Wells

Printed 26th May 1804, for Richard Phillips, Nº 71. St Pauls Church Yard.

51. This famous print purports to show Pantiles' personalities in 1748, in the summer of Nash's reign. Notice Thomas Loggan, the dwarf, who painted the picture, on the left under the colonnade.

52. Elizabeth Chudleigh, a celebrated 28-year-old beauty seen in the previous picture walking with Nash and Pitt, made her name the following year by appearing as Iphigenia in the costume shown here. She was already secretly married to the future Earl of Bristol (see below) but nevertheless married the Duke of Kingston bigamously in 1769.

53. Augustus Hervey, famous later as 'The English Casanova' and a bold and competent captain, was an impecunious naval lieutenant when he married Elizabeth Chudleigh in 1744 and sailed for the West Indies two days later. In 1775 he unexpectedly became Earl of Bristol. Local interest concerns the land owned by a later Earl which became Hervey Town (see plate 78).

54. Another romance with strong Tunbridge Wells associations was that between Lavinia Fenton and the Duke of Bolton. Lavinia was the first Polly Peachum in *The Beggar's Opera* in 1728 and the Duke watched night after night. Here in Hogarth's painting he is sitting third from the right. At the end of the season she became his mistress.

55. Having produced three sons, Lavinia eventually became Duchess of Bolton in 1751 when the first Duchess died. As mistress and wife, 'her conduct was notably discreet'. They settled in Tunbridge Wells where the Duke died in 1754 and the Dowager met an Irish doctor who cured her of a painful illness. When she died in 1760 he was her executor and residuary legatee.

56.   The Irish doctor was George Kelly. As executor he administered the Duchess's bequest of a clock (Polly Peachum's) for the chapel. By 1762 he had become Sir George, Lord of the Manor and substantial land-owner. In about 1765 he built for himself the house pictured here, later enlarged to become the present *Spa Hotel*. Lavinia's sons were said to be peeved.

57.   A letter in the Tunbridge Wells Museum, written by a milliner's assistant in 1754, describes the general excitement at Nash's arrival and her own disappointment at the sight of the great man. He was then 80 years old (he died in 1761) and this anonymous pencil sketch, inexplicably dated 1802, may be an accurate image of what she saw.

58. This wooden chapel was replaced in 1867 by Emmanuel Church, itself demolished in 1974 for hospital access. The original building, opened in July 1769 by George Whitefield, was sited in the grounds of the old Culverden House, then occupied by the Countess of Huntingdon who founded her own Nonconformist sect or 'Connexion'.

59. This 1772 painting by Richard Samuel shows how the pantiles were laid diagonally on the Upper Walk. By this date they were somewhat broken and were relaid with the present paving slabs in 1792. Note the Music Gallery in its old forward position. The building at the far end used to be the home of Loggan the artist.

60. For 10 weeks each year from 1769 until 1789, when he died, the Duke of Leeds rented Mount Pleasant House from William Gratton of the *Gloucester Tavern* who had married the widow of an owner subsequent to Lord Percival. The Duke is renowned for driving daily in his coach and six to a point on the turnpike he called Turnham (Turn 'em!) Green.

61. This 1793 painting by J. Green may be compared with the 1740 jacket illustration by Thomas Loggan. The viewpoint is similar. Lord Muskerry's arch has been much modified. The colonnade on the left seems to have been glazed in Loggan's time. The sundial has disappeared but the pantiles remain – despite the date, 1793.

62a. In 1898 this stone plaque was dug up in three pieces during preliminary building work at Lord Abergavenny's Home Farm Estate (Warwick Park). Having then narrowly escaped use as hard core, it is now displayed at the Grove Hill fire station.

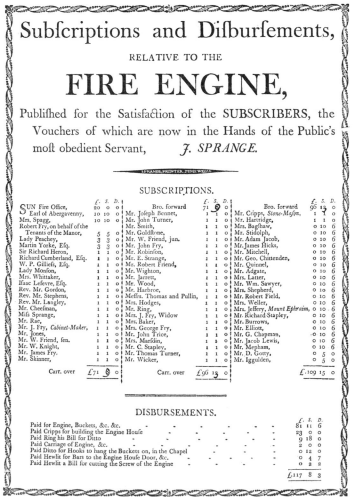

Subfcriptions and Difburfements,

RELATIVE TO THE

FIRE ENGINE,

Publifhed for the Satisfaction of the SUBSCRIBERS, the Vouchers of which are now in the Hands of the Public's moft obedient Servant,   *J. SPRANGE.*

SPRANGE, PRINTER, TUNB. WELLS.

SUBSCRIPTIONS.

	£	s.	d.		£	s.	d.		£	s.	d.
SUN Fire Office,	20	0	0	Bro. forward	71	9	0	Bro. forward	96	13	0
Earl of Abergavenny,	10	10	0	Mr. Joseph Bennet,	1	1	0	Mr. Cripps, *Stone-Mafon,*	1	1	0
Mrs. Spagg,	10	10	0	Mr. John Turner,	1	1	0	Mr. Hartridge,	1	1	0
Robert Fry, on behalf of the				Mr. Smith,	1	1	0	Mrs. Bagfhaw,	0	10	6
Tenants of the Manor,	5	5	0	Mr. Goldftone,	1	1	0	Mr. Stidolph,	0	10	6
Lady Peachey,	3	3	0	Mr. W. Friend, jun.	1	1	0	Mr. Adam Jacob,	0	10	6
Martin Yorke, Efq.	3	3	0	Mr. John Fry,	1	1	0	Mr. James Hicks,	0	10	6
Sir Richard Heron,	1	1	0	Mr. Robinfon,	1	1	0	Mr. Mitchell,	0	10	6
Richard Cumberland, Efq.	1	1	0	Mr. E. Strange,	1	1	0	Mr. Geo. Chittenden,	0	10	6
W. P. Gilliefs, Efq.	1	1	0	Mr. Robert Friend,	1	1	0	Mr. Quinnel,	0	10	6
Lady Monfon,	1	1	0	Mr. Wighton,	1	1	0	Mr. Adgate,	0	10	6
Mrs. Whittaker,	1	1	0	Mr. Jarrett,	1	1	0	Mrs. Latter,	0	10	6
Ifaac Lefevre, Efq.	1	1	0	Mr. Wood,	1	1	0	Mr. Wm. Sawyer,	0	10	6
Rev. Mr. Gordon,	1	1	0	Mr. Harbroe,	1	1	0	Mrs. Shepherd,	0	10	6
Rev. Mr. Stephens,	1	1	0	Meffrs. Thomas and Pullin,	1	1	0	Mr. Robert Field,	0	10	6
Rev. Mr. Langley,	1	1	0	Mrs. Hodges,	1	1	0	Mrs. Weller,	0	10	6
Mr. Cheefman,	1	1	0	Mr. Ring,	1	1	0	Mrs. Jeffery, *Mount Ephraim,*	0	10	6
Mifs Sprange,	1	1	0	Mrs. J. Fry, Widow	1	1	0	Mr. Richard Stapley,	0	10	6
Mr. Rae,	1	1	0	Mrs. Baker,	1	1	0	Mr. Burrows,	0	10	6
Mr. J. Fry, *Cabinet-Maker,*	1	1	0	Mrs. George Fry,	1	1	0	Mr. Elliott,	0	10	6
Mr. Jones,	1	1	0	Mrs. John Trice,	1	1	0	Mr. G. Chapman,	0	10	6
Mr. W. Friend, fen.	1	1	0	Mrs. Marfdin,	1	1	0	Mr. Jacob Lewis,	0	10	6
Mr. W. Knight,	1	1	0	Mr. C. Stapley,	1	1	0	Mr. Mepham,	0	10	6
Mr. James Fry.	1	1	0	Mr. Thomas Turner,	1	1	0	Mr. D. Gotty,	0	5	0
Mr. Skinner,	1	1	0	Mr. Wicker,	1	1	0	Mr. Iggulden,	0	5	0
Carr. over	£71	9	0	Carr. over	£96	13	0		£109	15	0

DISBURSEMENTS.

	£	s.	d.
Paid for Engine, Buckets, &c. &c.	81	11	6
Paid Cripps for building the Engine Houfe	23	0	0
Paid Ring his Bill for Ditto	9	18	0
Paid Carriage of Engine, &c.	2	0	0
Paid Ditto for Hooks to hang the Buckets on, in the Chapel	0	12	0
Paid Hewlit for Bars to the Engine Houfe Door, &c.	0	4	7
Paid Hewlit a Bill for cutting the Screw of the Engine	0	2	2
	£117	8	3

62b. Details of the event commemorated can be read on the Sprange poster: a veritable roll-call of contemporary citizenry.

The Waters of Scandal Recede
1800~24

63.   In 1802 the Lady of the Manor, Sir George Kelly's niece Elizabeth Shorey, laid 'the first stone of an elegant set of hot and cold baths, to be erected on a plan of the King's Surveyor' (*Maidstone Journal*, 11 May). The building, still there, can be recognised in this 1806 print published by Thomas Wise, the Tunbridge Ware maker.

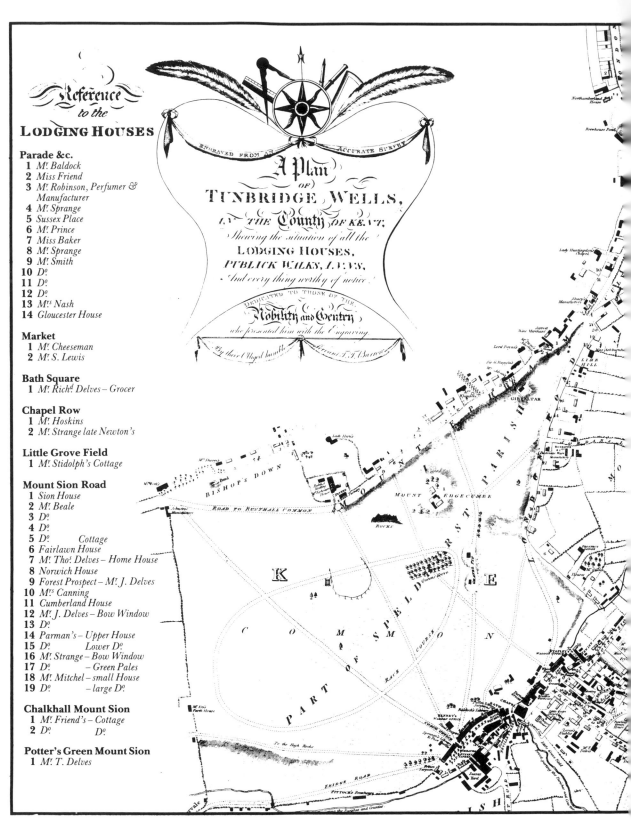

64. T. T. Barrow produced this invaluable map in 1808 and, curiously, located himself on it in the *Grove Tavern* building (see plate 43). However in 1810 he moved his business as 'Land Surveyor, House and Land Agent' to the London road. The map was then on sale, price 7s., at his office, at local libraries and at Hatchards, Piccadilly.

Remarks

Lodging Houses are distinguished thus ▦

Other Houses   thus ▪

Coach Houses, Stables &c.   thus ▨

When the trade is mentioned in the Reference the shop is near the Lodging House thus M.ʳ R. Delves, Grocer, &c.

A *By the Bath, Nash, Stationer*
B *Duke of York, Public House*
C *Coach and Horse, D.º*
A *By Sion Crescent, Fry's Boarding School*

Reference *to the* LODGING HOUSES

Sion Place
1 *Bowling Green House*
2 *M.ᵗˢ Wood*
3 *Miss Wood*
4 *D.º*
5 *M.ʳ John Fry – Union Hall*

Sion Crescent
1 *Miss Baker – Great House*
2 *D.º – Middle D.º*
3 *M.ʳ Gilbert*

Crescent Passage M! Sion
1 *M.ʳ Peerless – Glover &c.*
2 *Parman's – Cottage*

Grove Mount Sion
1 *First Grove House – Miss Fry*
2 *North Grove D.º Dowager Lady Deering*

Little Grove M! Sion
1 *Little Grove House*
2 *D.º*

Foot *of* Mount Sion
1 *Chapel House*
2 *M.ʳ J. Fry – Manufacturer &c.*
3 *M.ʳ Peerless*
4 *M.ʳ J. Fry*
5 *Roseberry House – M.ʳ Stapley*
6 *M.ʳ Smith*
7 *M.ʳ J. Delves, late Philpots*
8 *M.ʳ Parsons*
9 *M.ʳ Friend's Cottage*
10 *M.ʳ Hunter*
11 *D.º*
12 *M.ʳ Hunter*
13 *M.ʳ Elliott*
14 *Merrivale*
15 *D.º*
16 *First New Street House* }
17 *Great New Street D.º* } *M.ʳ Skinner*
18 *Corner New Street D.º* }
19 *M.ʳ Stapley*
20 *M.ʳ Hayward – Wine Merchant*
21 *M.ʳ Stapley – Carrier*

London Road
1 *Little Bath House* }
2 *Middle Bath D.º* } *M.ʳ Skinner*
3 *Great Bath D.º* }
4 *Heath Cottage* }
5 *Sydenham House* } *M.ʳ Howe*
6 *M.ᵗˢ Hartridge*
7 *Vale Royal* }
8 *D.º* } *M.ʳ Skinner*
9 *Little Holly Bush* }
10 *Great Holly Bush* }

11 *Rose Hill, M.ʳ Rae*
12 *Jordan House – M.ʳ Burrows*
13 *M.ᵗˢ Jeffery*
14 *M.ᵗˢ Sawyer – Glazier*
15 *Summer Hill – M.ᵗˢ Gower*
16 *M.ʳ Pope*
17 *M.ʳ Knott*
18 *Rock Cottage* }
19 *Miss Latters* } *Late Miss Latters*
20 *M.ᵗˢ Cranwell*
21 *M.ʳ Morfett*

Culverden
1 *M.ʳ Morfett*
2 *Culverden House – M.ᵗˢ Bullien*
3 *M.ʳ T. Sawyer*
4 *M.ᵗˢ J. Delves, – late Weller's*
5 *D.º – upper House*
6 *M.ᵗˢ Langridge*
7 *M.ʳ Knight*
8 *M.ʳ Langridge*
9 *M.ʳ Panuwell's – Cottage*
10 *D.º Great House*

Culverden Row
1 *M.ʳ Nye – Baker*
2 *M.ʳ Nye – Taylor*
3 *M.ᵗˢ Latter*
4 *M.ᵗˢ Hayward*

Mount Pleasant
1 *Great Mount Pleasant*
2 *D.º*
3 *M.ᵗˢ Marsden*
4 *M.ʳ Dudley*
5 *M.ʳ Maryan*
6 *Little Mount Pleasant*

Jordon's Lane
1 *M.ʳ Morley*

Mount Edgecumbe
1 *M.ʳ Bennett*
2 *M.ʳ Sawyer*

Mount Ephraim
1 *M.ᵗˢ Jarrett*
2 *M.ʳ Stone*
3 *D.º*
4 *Stone House*
5 *M.ʳ Chapman*
6 *M.ᵗˢ Whittaker*
7 *Castle House*
8 *M.ʳ Simpson*
9 *M.ʳ Richardson*

Bishop's Down
1 *White House*
2 *Little Grove D.º*
3 *M.ʳ Chapman*
4 *M.ᵗˢ Shorey's – Great House*
5 *D.º lower house*

Summer Vale
M.ʳ Moon

Road *to* London *beyond the* Culverden
1 *Northumberland House. M.ʳ R. Strange*
2 *Percy Cottage*

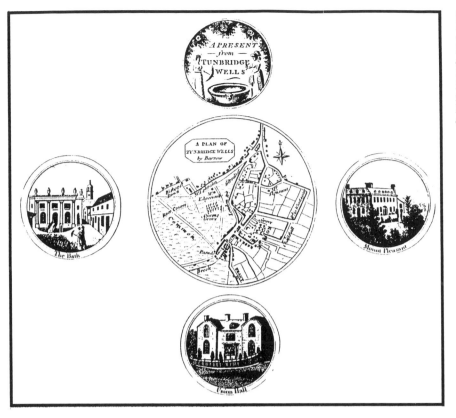

65. This design by map-maker Barrow, presumably intended as wrapping paper for that little home-coming gift or souvenir piece of Tunbridge Ware, shows the new Bath House, Mount Pleasant House (*Calverley Hotel*), and, most interestingly, General Murray's house in Berkeley Road, then called Union Hall.

66. This 1690s' house, photographed by David Johnson in 1934, has been called Sion House for more than 100 years but, confusingly, the house opposite (Bedford Place, now demolished) was called Sion House on Barrow's map and the house pictured here was called Green Pales. It was then a lodging house run by Edward Strange, of the well-known local family.

67. Richard Cumberland (1732-1811), dramatist and Board of Trade Secretary, went on a secret mission to Lisbon in 1780 and was never reimbursed. He settled modestly in Cumberland House on the old Mount Sion Bowling Green. Henry Fry, owner of this portrait, was his loyal lieutenant in the Volunteer Infantry which Cumberland commanded during the Napoleonic scare.

68. Richard Cumberland had three daughters and four sons. Charles, here aged about seven, became an All-England fast bowler, and lived for a time near his father. A brother-in-law, Lord Edward Bentinck, shared his cricketing enthusiasm. They gave the successful players a hat each after a match on the Common in 1786!

Drawn by De Wilde.   Published by H. Berthoud Jun.r Sept.r 16.th 1820.   Engraved by R. Cooper.

(as Doctor Cantwell) M.r DOWTON, (in the Hypocrite.)

Alas Madam! I am not a good man. Act.1.st Scene 5.th

69. William Dowton made his reputation playing the name part in Richard Cumberland's *The Jew* at Drury Lane in 1796. He had strong local connections, joining Mrs. Baker's company in 1791 and marrying her daughter. He, and later his son, managed her theatre on the Pantiles from 1815 to 1838. He played 'Cantwell' at the Lyceum in 1810.

70. This print must, by a little, post-date 1811 when Bedford Place, on the left, was still called Sion House (see plate 66). Between it and the chapel, in the background, is Chapel House, a large boarding house sometimes known as 'Bedlam'! On the right is probably the building marked 'Fry's Cabinet Warehouse' on Barrow's map. (See also plates 121 and 126.)

71. Paul Amsinck took over as Master of Ceremonies in 1805 and in 1810 wrote and illustrated an informative book, *Tunbridge Wells and Neighbourhood*, from which this drawing of the Vale Royal corner of the London Road is taken, demonstrating the scattered houses and the rural nature of the scene. The Grove Houses front the trees of the Grove.

72. The original drawing for this print was exhibited in 1809. The model for Hebe, serving nectar to eagle Jupiter, is thought to be Madame Caballero who bought Grecian Villa in 1834. According to W. C. Cripps, her solicitor when she was old, she was the Poll Raffles whose liaison with the Marquess Wellesley was a matter of Regency gossip, although local legend connects her with the younger brother, the Duke of Wellington.

Jupiter as eagle

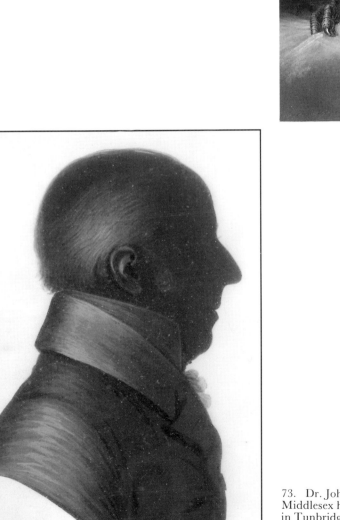

Mayo

73. Dr. John Mayo, physician to the Foundling and Middlesex hospitals, also had a flourishing summer practice in Tunbridge Wells and a house (see plate 112) on Mount Ephraim. The future Duchess of Wellington was his patient in Tunbridge Wells in 1810 and also in London. He died in 1818 and left his practice in Tunbridge Wells to his son Thomas (see plate 90).

the Duke of Sussex's House Bag Tunbridge 1821

74. Wellington Place, named after a supposed sojourn of the future Duchess in 1809 and recently renovated after a fire, was built according to Colbran (1840) by Sir George Buggins (see plate 64). The caption, unidentified but probably trustworthy, links it with George IV's brother, who was present the previous year at a ball celebrating Queen Caroline's adultery acquittal.

75. Brick-making was a common local industry, in Tunbridge Wells as elsewhere, and continued until the closure of the High Brooms works (1885-1968). This sketch by a visitor in 1824 gives an impression of the methods of that time. The brick kiln on the London Road is probably that shown on the Bowra map opposite the brewery (the present telephone exchange).

Brick kiln on the London Road.

76.   Brewing was another local industry. Many large houses once had their own brewhouses, but there were also commercial ones: this one on the Eridge Road (called Newnham's on Bowra, Pittock's on Barrow, and later the Victoria Brewery); the central one (see plate 96); and the St John's Road one, later Kelsey's. Again our anonymous visitor has provided a vivid 1824 impression.

77.   The Sand Caves, used for the extraction of fine sand and extending deep into the hillside, were once a well-known sight on entering the town from London but the road has been heightened and the caves blocked (see also plate 160). On the left in our visitor's 1824 sketch must be Gibraltar Cottage; the castellated house on the right still exists.

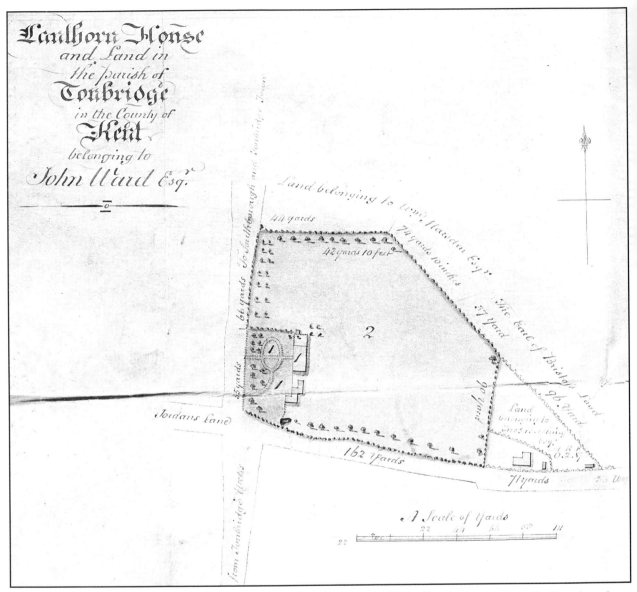

Lanthorn House and Land in the parish of Tonbridge in the County of Kent belonging to John Ward Esq.

Land belonging to Wm. Hawden Esq.

To Sadlhurough and Tonbridge Town

The Earl of Bristols Land

44 yards

42 yards 10 feet

74 yards 10 inches

66 yards

37 yard

2

96 yard

Land belonging to Jordans Land

55 yards

Land belonging to Ino. meeting Esq.

162 yards

71 yards

from Tonbridge Wells

A Scale of Yards

78. The Lanthorn House, demolished about 1828, occupied the present Town Hall site before Calverley Parade and Terrace. Possibly the house which John Brett left to his widow in 1719, it was certainly the home of his great-nephew, Rev. John Brett, until 1787. This legal plan is all that survives today. Notice the Earl of Bristol's land.

The Calverley Development
1825~40

79.   The first stage of the Calverley development was Holy Trinity Church, consecrated in 1829. Here the royal party rides past the church, perhaps in 1834. The road was then called Jordans Lane after the house at the other end (see plate 27). Beyond the church can be seen balconied Dorset House, Place and Villa, now replaced by office blocks.

Calverley Parade, Tunbridge Wells

80. This pair of notepaper illustrations shows Decimus Burton's Calverley Parade and Terrace which, facing west and south respectively, replaced the ancient Lanthorn House and its meadow in about 1830. Local residents (as one complained in the newspaper) were struck with dismay at the huge stone walls and rows of houses 'ycleped parades and terraces, and colonnades and crescents'!

Calverley Terrace, Tunbridge Wells.

Sketched by T.H. Clarke

J.S. Templeton lith.

VILLAS IN CALVERLEY PARK.

London, Published by J.BRITTON Augs.t 1831.

81. As can be seen, the villas of Calverley Park were largely completed by 1831. They form the most admired and influential part of Burton's development. This print demonstrates that the Park has not lost too much of its character. The Victoria Gate can also be seen, with the Terrace beyond and Mount Pleasant (Calverley) House showing below the church tower.

82. This looks like an architect's impression but shows clearly what Burton in fact built to form his 'commercial' Calverley Road. All that remains now are some altered parts of Calverley Place. The market was opened in 1840 but by 1846 had become the Town Hall for the new Commissioners (see plate 161).

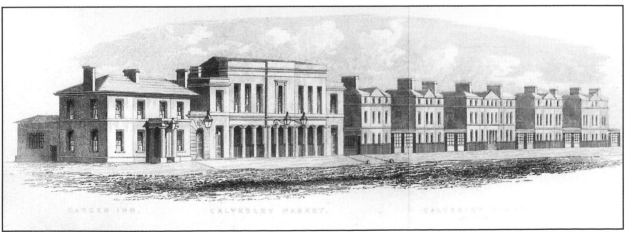

GARDEN INN.   CALVERLEY MARKET.   CALVERLEY

83. Great Culverden House, one of the local works of Decimus Burton outside the Calverley Estate, was built in 1829-30 on the site of the house in whose grounds the Countess of Huntingdon had built her chapel (see plate 58). This is why Emmanuel Church, which replaced the chapel, was (until demolished) next door to the hospital, which replaced the house.

84. This painting from the Museum Collection is dated 30 September 1830. It shows the nowadays busy junction of the London, Frant and Eridge roads with the Chapel of King Charles the Martyr on the left, and the entrance to the Pantiles on the right. On the extreme right is the back of the 1804 Bath House (see plate 63) and to its left Pelham House, occupied by the Delves House Agency, more concerned in those days with letting than selling.

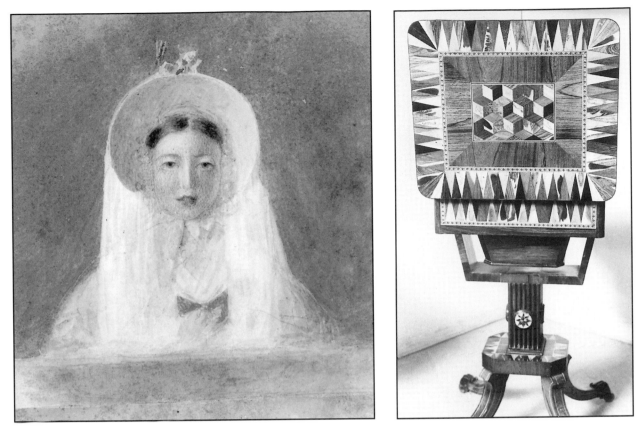

85. (*Above left*) While the Calverley development was going on, Princess Victoria and her mother, the Duchess of Kent, were regular summer visitors. What the Princess thought of it all is unclear: we do know, however, that she did not think the Rev. Pope's sermon on 24 August 1834 as good as some of his others. This delightful sketch shows her on that occasion.

86. (*Above right*) The one industry special to the locality was Tunbridge Ware: an obvious choice, therefore, for a seventh birthday gift from the town to Princess Victoria in 1826. Messrs. R. Mercer, J. Thomas and Richard Delves formed the presentation committee and William Fenner did the work. The original combined writing-desk and workbox is unfortunately mislaid; the workbox illustrated, from the Museum Collection, with the lid open to show the mosaic, is not dissimilar.

87. The Duchess of Kent and Princess Victoria spent the night of 3/4 November 1834 at the *Sussex Hotel* before leaving, as depicted here, on the long coach ride to St Leonard's-on-Sea. Since the Duchess had Decimus Burton to dinner during her stay at the Wells, is it impossible that he persuaded her to patronise his father James's newly-developed seaside resort?

88. Rev. William Law Pope was minister at King Charles' from 1829 to 1879. An Irishman (as appears from a court report) and a bachelor, he lived after 1846 in a new villa in Eden Road. Among his good works were the job-creating Brighton Lake or 'Pope's Puddle', and the foundation of Murray House Girls' School.

89. Lord Percival's old Mount Pleasant House was bought by John Ward, the Calverley developer, in 1825 but remained unaltered while required by the Duchess of Kent. In 1837 however it was enlarged with 'two elegant wings' and an additional storey (to make 50 bedchambers and 14 sitting-rooms) and in 1839 it was leased to Edward Churchill, landlord of the *Kentish Royal*.

90. Thomas Mayo (1790-1871), son of John Mayo, was a distinguished doctor, becoming President of the Royal College of Physicians from 1857 to 1862. He continued his father's practice in Tunbridge Wells until 1835 when he settled in Wimpole Street, selling the house he had built in 1824 to Madame Caballero (see plates 72 and 118) who called it Grecian Villa.

91. The crescent of houses called Grove Hill Gardens, facing the Grove Bowling Club (established in its gardens in 1909) and backing onto Claremont Road, was built shortly after Calverley Park. This detail from an unattributed painting in the Museum Collection shows the part-completed group. More interestingly, it reveals in the right-hand background the only glimpse we have of Grecian Villa.

THE SPHYNX;

OR

Tunbridge Wells Instructor.

Vol. I. No. 1. THURSDAY 26, Nov. 1835. *Price* 1d.

THE

MEETING OF COMMISSIONERS,

A VISION.

Let any of your two-legged, fourteen-stone animals who ride donkeys, say what they please, I am fully persuaded that donkeys have feelings and are rational beings; infinitely superior to those who drive them, and very little inferior in taste and sentiment to the he and she bipeds who ride them.

92.   The *Sphynx* or *Tunbridge Wells Instructor* tried perhaps to fill the gap left by closure of *The Visitor* which ran from 1833 to 1835. Its first issue came shortly after the inauguration of the Town Commissioners under the Improvement Act of 1835; maybe the new commissioners were not amused! The *Sphynx* did not last long anyway.

93.   This part of a wider panorama (about 1840) shows, probably reasonably accurately, the chapel on the extreme right; Bedford Place and Jerningham House; Roseberry (Martins Lower) House at the bottom of Little Mount Sion and Philip Seale's houses further up; the row, including the *Compasses*, flanking the Grove, and much more that may be puzzled out from Barrow's Map.

The Coming of the Railway
1841-59

Part of the High Rocks near Tunbridge Wells.

94.   The lines inscribed on one of the 'High Rocks', commencing 'O Infidel ...', were written by James Phippen, best known as editor of Colbran's early guides. He had a bookshop next to York House in the High Street and was local correspondent for the *Sussex Agricultural Express*. His account of the dinner following the planting of the Queen's Grove in 1835 is worth reading.

95. The present hospital had its origins in a dispensary established by local people in the High Street (exact position uncertain) in 1828. In 1842 it moved to this handsome building in Grosvenor Road which was enlarged by stages to form the General Hospital.

96. The Mount Pleasant Brewery was started by William Baines who leased the site in December 1689. He died in 1720 and the brewery passed to William King. Robert Friend and his descendants had it from 1750 until at least 1808. It had become Bell's Brewery by 1845 when it was demolished to make way for the Central Station.

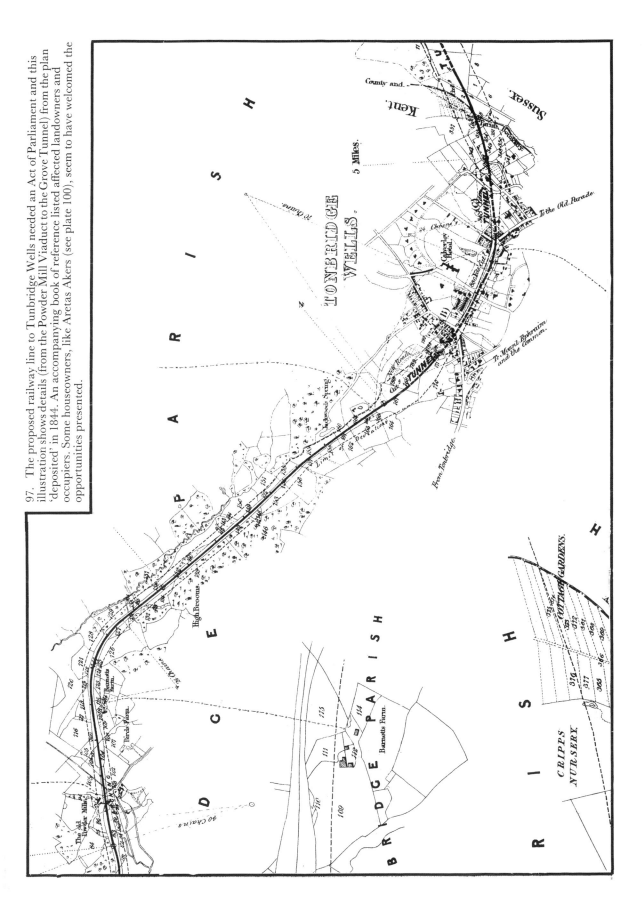

97. The proposed railway line to Tunbridge Wells needed an Act of Parliament and this illustration shows details (from the Powder Mill Viaduct to the Grove Tunnel) from the plan 'deposited' in 1844. An accompanying book of reference listed affected landowners and occupiers. Some houseowners, like Aretas Akers (see plate 100), seem to have welcomed the opportunities presented.

98.   The South Eastern Railway was formed in 1836 to build a line from London to Dover; it reached Tonbridge in 1842 and Dover in 1844. Tunbridge Wells was a branch from this line and first terminated at the 'Jack Woods Spring' (old Goods) Station. On the way it had to cross the valley of the 18th-century powder mill.

99.   The railway line reached the Central Station in 1845 and by the date of this print, August 1851, had not quite arrived at Hastings. The train is going that way, under the footbridge which still exists between the Banner Farm Estate, on the right, and Upper Cumberland Walk. The double bow-fronted building must be Cecil Court, with Belle Vue on the right.

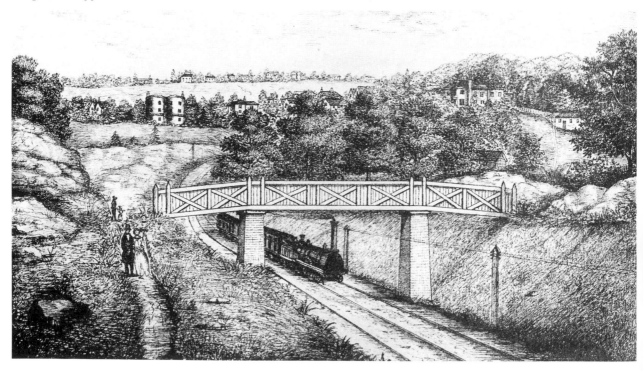

100. Aretas Akers Esquire lived in Belle Vue House from about 1830 to 1845, many of his children being baptised at King Charles' Chapel. Retiring from the bar owing to ill-health, he was a magistrate and active participant in local affairs. He edited a family magazine from which this drawing is taken. A grandson became Lord Chilston in 1911.

101. Part of John Brett's estate in 1738, Belle Vue House belonged to John Lloyd when he died in 1826. Aretas Akers, who never liked it, was having alterations made by Decimus Burton when he sold it in 1845 to the South Eastern Railway which demolished it in the 1850s. This painting is by one of the children who loved it.

102. Queen Victoria's mother, the Duchess of Kent, was perhaps the greatest royal patroness of Tunbridge Wells, through her visits with her daughter between 1826 and 1835, and her final visit in 1849. Certainly her patronage was for long the pride of many local businesses and her charity was not confined to the years of her visits.

103. The Duchess of Kent stayed from August to October 1849 at Eden House, seen here before demolition in 1969. On her birthday, 17 August, a procession of 2,000 children and municipal dignitaries marched past. She was not, however, as legend states, visited by her daughter, since Queen Victoria and Prince Albert's day trip took place on 23 June.

104. This must be the earliest photograph of the Pantiles, if not of the town. It was taken in 1851 by John Cumming (see plates 105 and 106) or one of his family, using the calotype process. The scene is noticeably deserted, but it was taken out of season as proved by the leafless trees, no doubt because the presence of moving people had to be avoided.

105. Another Cumming photograph, dated 1854, shows Kentish Cottage from the Eridge Road at Roper's Gate (Garden Centre corner). The gentleman in the topper is standing on the bridge over the River Grom. Cumming was a Scottish minister with a church in Covent Garden who relaxed by keeping bees at Kentish Cottage, his 'Beemaster' letters to *The Times* becoming celebrated.

106. A third Cumming photograph bears the caption 'First houses in Nevill Park. Haystack where Mrs. Elsley's Tennis Court now is – children of our family – with grownup – all Churchill's Farm'. Churchill's was perhaps Hungershall Farm and the site of the tennis court can still be seen outlined by trees. The reference to tennis means the caption must have been added later.

Expansion: 1860~88

107. This drawing shows the busy Vale Road Post Office corner as it was in the mid-19th century.
Mr. Cramp (mentioned by Thackeray in the *Roundabout Papers*) ran his horse-riding business from Bath Yard
(now Vale Road), to the left of the building with the cart outside. On the far left is Sydenham Villa where the
future Duchess of Wellington stayed in 1810.

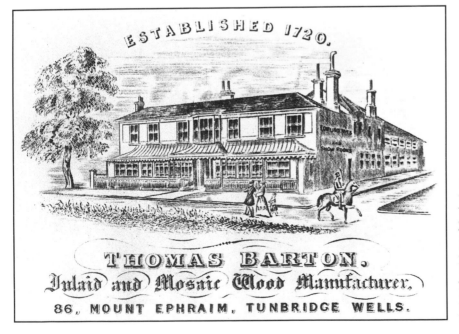

ESTABLISHED 1720.

THOMAS BARTON,
Inlaid and Mosaic Wood Manufacturer,
86, MOUNT EPHRAIM, TUNBRIDGE WELLS.

108. This letterhead demonstrates
that this pretty Mount Ephraim
villa was indeed the late 19th-
century Tunbridge Ware factory.
Thomas Barton worked for
Edmund Nye as designer and
partner, took over the Mount
Ephraim manufactory on Nye's
death in 1863 and was active un[til]
he died in 1902. The Fenners, w[ho]
preceded Nye, claimed the fac[tory]
was established in 1720.

109. Dr. Webber, who caused the 1864 riots, became local director of a company unsuccessfully floated to rebuild the *Kentish Royal Hotel*. This uncaptioned cartoon, from the papers of the late Mr. Pratley of Hall's Bookshop, shows the hotel entrance, a notice 'Site for New Hotel', Dr. Webber in a donkey cart, and (shouldering tools) possibly the Town Surveyor, Mr. Wright.

110. This photograph of the London-Tunbridge Wells coach was probably taken some years after Dr. Webber's adventures, but clearly visible is the *Kentish Royal Hotel* porch where on Wednesday 20 July the doctor threatened to put the contents of his seven-barrelled revolver through the heart of jeweller Thomas Kinlan of Chapel Place, one of his persecutors.

111.   Did the Webber riots prompt the *London Illustrated News* to publish on 21 September 1864 this animated engraving of citizens and visitors 'promenading' on the Pantiles, as if to rejoice at the doctor's departure? The affair had reached the national newspapers in August. Notice that Nos. 12 to 16 (see plate 19) were the Post Office, run by William Nash.

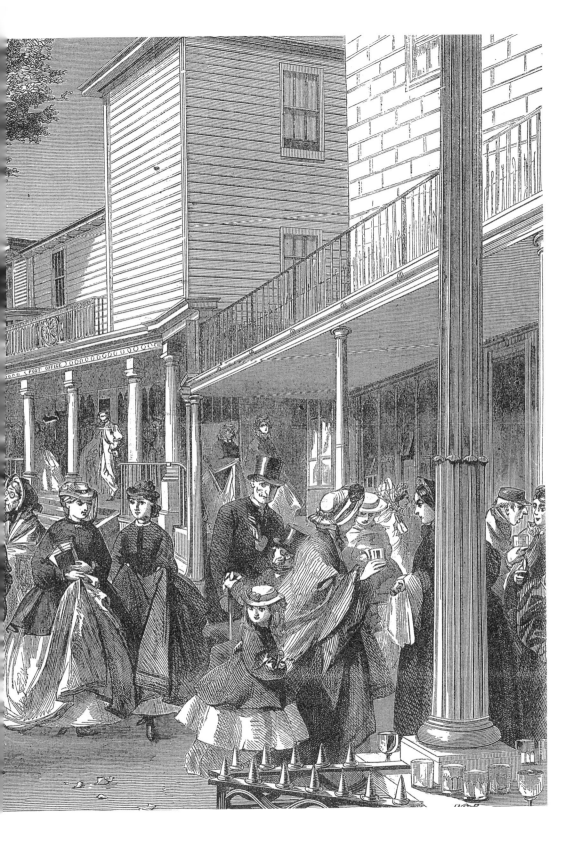

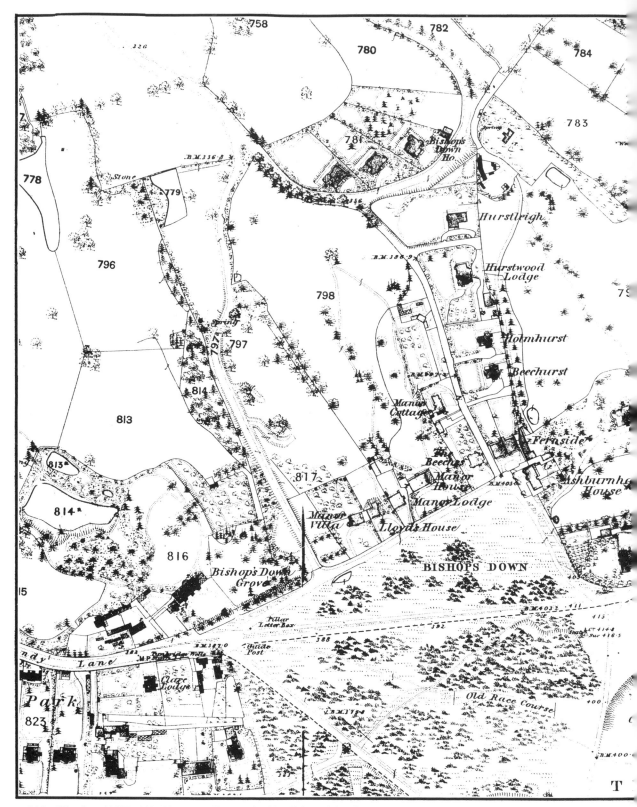

112. The first (1867, 1/2500 or 25 miles per inch) edition of the Ordnance Survey was arranged by parishes. Since the boundary between Speldhurst and Tonbridge parishes almost bisects the town, separate illustrations are needed for the two parishes. The Speldhurst parish map (a section only) is of particular interest in showing and naming the houses along Mount Ephraim.

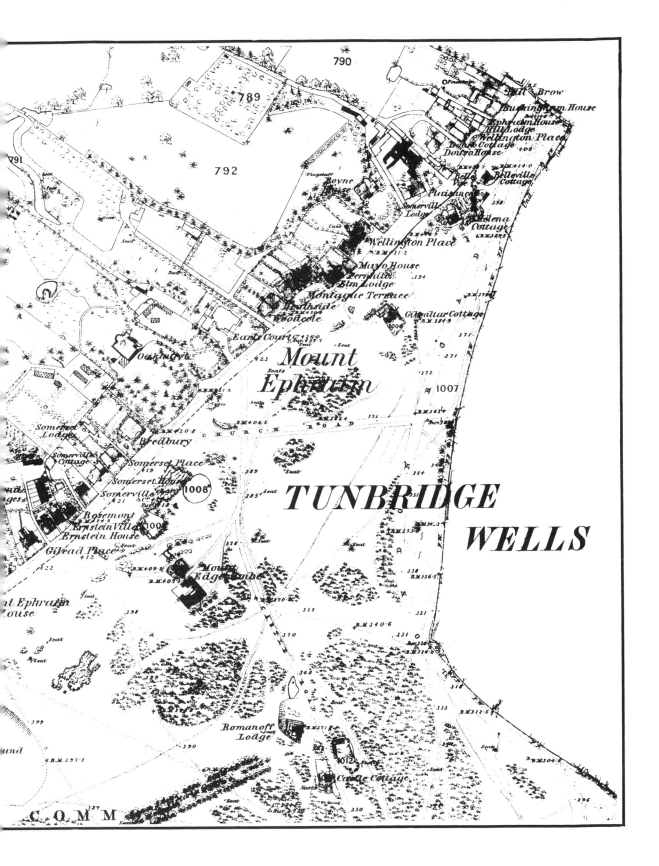

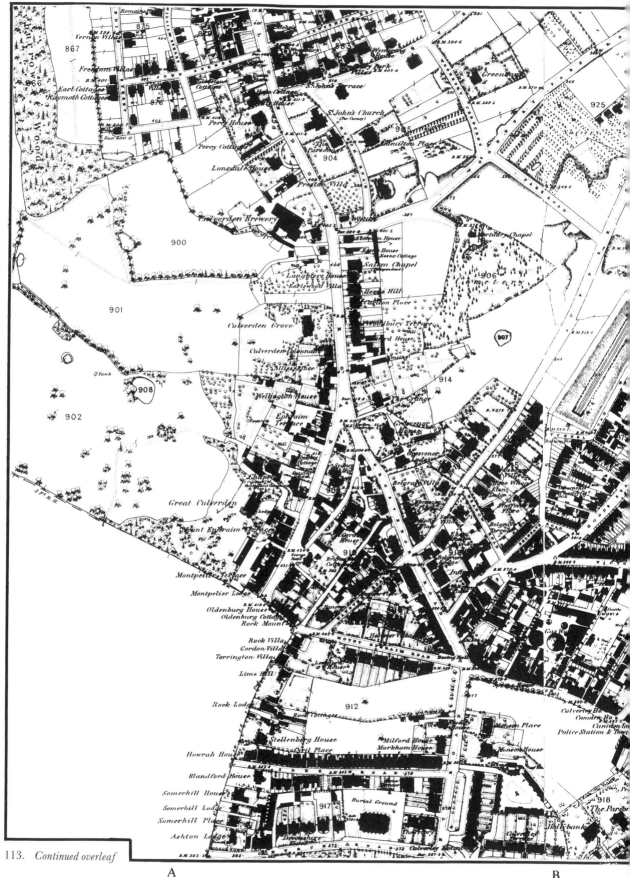

867

866

Vernon Villas

Freedom Villas

Earl Cottages
Reymoth Cottages

875

876

Percy House

Percy Cottages

Lonsdale House

Preston Villa

900

901

902

908

907

906

Culverden Brewery

Culverden Grove

Culverden Columna

Culverden Colonnade

Wellington House

Ephraim Terrace

Great Culverden

Mount Ephraim

Montpelier Terrace

Montpelier Lodge

Oldenburg House
Oldenburg Cottage
Rock Mount

Rock Villa
Gordon Villa
Torrington Villas

Lime Hill

Rock Lodge

Rock Cottages

912

Stellenberg House
Orib Place

Howrah House

Blandford House

Somerhill House
Somerhill Lodge
Somerhill Place

Ashton Lodge

917

Burial Ground

St John's Terrace

St John's Church

Hamilton Place

904

925

905

Salem Chapel

Hessle Hill

Fruiston Place

Woodbury Terrace

914

The Grange

Grosvenor

Grosvenor

Belgrave Villa

918

Garden House

918

Hanover

Milford House
Markham House

Manson Place

Manson House

925

Calverley Ho
Camden Ho
Camden In
Police Station & Town

918

The Parso

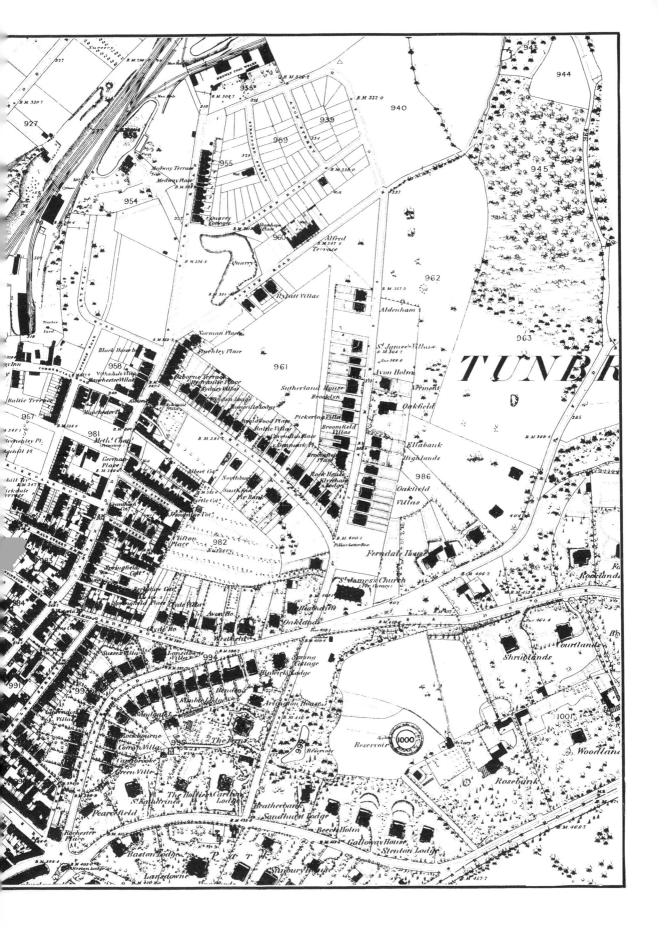

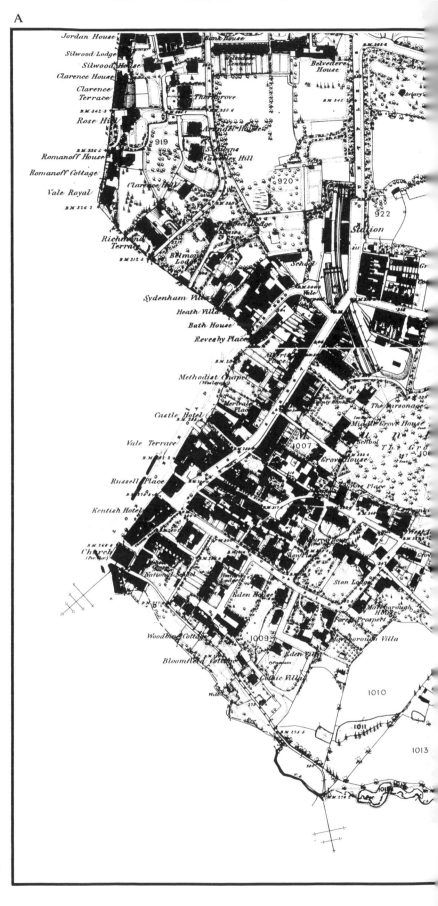

A

113. This section of the Tonbridge parish map shows most of what would be considered the centre of the town and enables many buildings, some of which have been illustrated, to be located: for example, Calverley Parade and Terrace, the dispensary, Monson Place and House, the old gas works etc. The house names down the London road are also of interest.

114. This photograph of the fishmarket in about 1870 harks back to the days when the gentry shopped on the Pantiles for their dinners, as Celia Fiennes noticed in 1697. The fishmarket is shown on the earliest plan made in 1725, but the building dates from later in the 18th century. Tolsons were there from the 1840s to 1920s.

115. William Henry Delves (1829-1922) joined the Tunbridge Wells Rifle Volunteers in 1859, and by 1873 was colour sergeant and a crack shot. In civilian life he was manager of Molineux, Whitfield & Co.'s 'Old Bank' on the Parade, chairman of the gas company 1889-1920 and mayor in 1900-1 when he laid the foundation stone for the Opera House.

116. The lower yard opposite the *Royal Sussex Hotel* used to be much wider. This photograph shows a later development with a sloping bank planted with shrubs and must date from before 1877 when the Pump Room was built. Henry Steed was landlord in 1874, and the hotel closed in 1880.

117. The Great Hall (on the left), opening in 1870, about six years before this photograph was taken, served as playhouse, concert hall and assembly hall. It was later a cinema and a night club before being gutted by fire. In danger of demolition, it has risen from the ashes as a shopping arcade and offices. Notice the station clock tower and bridge, both later replaced.

118. Madame Caballero (see plates 72 and 90), photographed here in later life, lived sometimes in London and sometimes at Grecian Villa until about 1870 when she settled at neighbouring Claremont Lodge. When she died in 1877 she bequeathed Grecian Villa to her doctor, Frederick Manser, who soon disposed of it for housing development – hence Buckingham, Grecian and Norfolk Roads.

119. The dairy that still serves most of the town began when John Brown started a 'milk walk' from the back of Sion House. He then moved to Woods Cottage (with the weather-boarding and half-hipped roof), next to Berkeley Place on Mount Sion. This photograph shows milkmen assembling in about 1880. By 1888 the tree had been replaced by a purpose-built dairy.

120. Anyone walking up Grosvenor Road can see Grosvenor Lodge, just below the fishmonger's. Part of the Grosvenor Estate bought by Richard Delves on George Weller's death in 1785 and descending by inheritance to son-in-law James Hockett Fry and his son, Rev. James Fry, who sold up, it was the home of the artist C. T. Dodd junior, seen here with his family.

121. The entrance to Chapel Place has changed beyond recognition. On the left, where the fishmonger's now is, straggly trees mark the garden of Walmer House/Bedford Place (compare with plate 70). The faint outline of the present Kentish Mansions above shows that the photograph must date from after 1878.

122. Gas production started in 1835 in Golden Lane, now Golding Street (see plate 113). In 1845 a company of local shareholders, chaired by Joseph Delves of Mount Sion, took over from the original entrepreneur, W. J. Berry. Demand expanded and in 1880 new works were erected, despite opposition, in a 'seqestered valley' at High Brooms. They closed in 1967, although two gasholders remain.

The Charter Years: 1889-1909

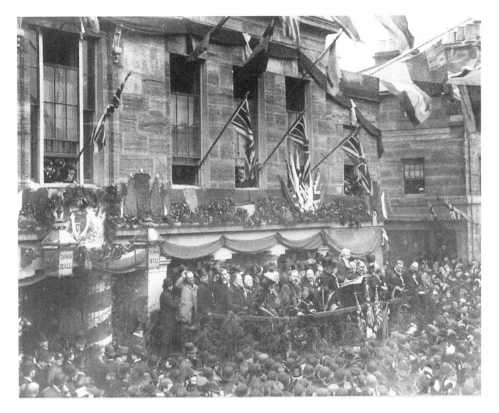

123. In this well-known but historically interesting photograph the man in the lawyer's wig reading the town's charter outside the Town Hall (the old Market Hall in Calverley Road – see plates 82 and 161) on 27 February 1889 is the first town clerk, William Charles Cripps, who was to serve with distinction for 36 years.

124. Plain J. S. Wigg was already an active Town Commissioner in 1864, taking part in the debates aroused by Dr. Webber. By 1888 John Stone-Wigg was chairman and the following year became the first mayor of the new borough, paying personally the legal costs of the charter and buying his mayoral chain. Henry Peach Robinson, the nationally famous local photographer, made this portrait.

125. About 1888 the sloping bank (seen in plate 116) was replaced by the present high stone wall and public conveniences were constructed underneath. There was an outcry and the trustees of Col. Weller, late Lord of the Manor, and his widow sued the Corporation, citing the Rusthall Manor Act of 1739. The House of Lords spent two days in 1896 discussing, among much else, the Boghouse on Kip's engraving and the 'Passing Houses' mentioned in the Manor Act. The Corporation lost but the conveniences lingered until the latest redevelopment.

126. Walmer House with Bedford Place (see plate 70) formed one building at the bottom of Mount Sion, dating from about 1735. In about 1889 it became the Technical Institute, as pictured here, before the Institute moved to the new building in Monson Road in 1902. A row of shop fronts then disguised the old building behind, until everything was demolished in 1973.

127.   Electricity arrived in 1895 when, during the mayoralty of Sir David Salomons, a municipal power station was built on the old quarry site alongside the Goods Station. The plant, substantially extended in 1925, closed in 1969. Here we see the cooling towers and one ornate chimney (now gone), the turbine house (still standing) and, behind, the mass of St Barnabas' Church.

128.   The first Motor Show in England was held on the Agricultural Showground in 1895, organised by Sir David Salomons. Perhaps it provided the inspiration for this car. According to a note on the photograph, it was 'built in 1900 in Grove Hill Road by Mr. E. Powell'. 'E. Powell, electrical, motor and cycle engineer' traded from No. 10 Grove Hill Road in 1907.

129. The identity of this mounted band and the occasion of its parade in front of the Church of King Charles are unknown. Of interest is the weather-boarded greengrocer's shop beyond the leading bandsman, demolished in 1900 to make way for the bank on the corner. To its right, with the blind, is Hall's Bookshop.

130. Monson House dated from before 1738 and Monson Place, next door, was built between 1808 and 1839. Both houses were demolished in 1898 to make way for the Opera House. David Johnson was tipped off to take this photograph by Dr. Abbott (see plate 133) and later took soil photographs for him when the foundations were dug out.

131.   The foundation stone of the Opera House was laid on 10 October 1901 by Mayor W. H. Delves and Sir H. Beerbohm Tree. Opened in 1902, it played host in early years to Paderewski, Melba, Clara Butt and Sir Frank Benson (see below). Nowadays the magnificent interior echoes only to the voice of the bingo-caller.

132.   A little boy born at Eden House in 1858 became an actor and later Sir Frank Benson who toured the country with his Shakespearian Company and played frequently at the Opera House in the town of his birth. This signed photograph of Benson as Hamlet was taken probably about 1900 in County Cork.

133. Surgeon to the Eye and Ear Hospital before it moved to Mount Sion (see plate 151),
Dr. George Abbott pursued interests in Technical Education and geology on retirement. From
1898 David Johnson helped him, taking photographs and carrying his equipment on geological
expeditions. Here the doctor is demonstrating the Tunbridge Wells sandstone strata. In the
background is Boyne Tower, No. 12 Boyne Park, built in 1895.

134. The signboard for Renault and Rover cars contradicts the dominance of the horse in this Edwardian postcard view
of the bottom of Grove Hill Road.

135. Mayor William Henry Delves seems, in this 1901 photograph, to have moved the paper from which he was reading the proclamation of the accession of King Edward VII. The scene is the balcony of Nos. 30-2 The Pantiles (see plate 153). It was this king who in 1909 was graciously pleased to bestow the title 'Royal' on Tunbridge Wells.

136. Taken by David Johnson about 1900, this photograph shows the old station clock tower, replaced by the present one in 1911-12. On the right, with the ornate lantern, is the *Railway Bell Hotel* which was acquired by Weekes and demolished in 1912. The prominent building behind the clock tower was *Lonsdale Mansions* (see plate 142), a private hotel.

137. 'What the ocean is to a sea-bathing town, that the Common is to Tunbridge Wells' used to be the saying, exemplified in this postcard of 1906, one among many to be entitled 'Sunday afternoon on the Common'. Nowadays the seaside and other distractions are but a short drive away and the Common is deserted.

138. The *Blue Anchor Inn*, the ivy-covered building in the background of this Edwardian postcard, was bequeathed by Nicholas Wood to his daughter Susanna in 1724. An inn until about 1778 and then a private house, it was demolished in 1933. The terrace on the left, designed by architects Weekes and Hughes in about 1877, flanks the site of the old Mount Sion Bowling Green.

139. The weather-boarded attic (top right) housed the first photographic studio in Tunbridge Wells, established by George Lawrence in 1860. Later the corner building was used by Luck & Hatt, then Walter Luck alone until 1895, followed by George Glanville until 1900. Later still came Cousens, Doyle Rowe, Minto and lastly Summerfield. A bank replaced the corner building in 1927. Notice the old dairy cart.

The World Wars: 1911-1944

140. On 22 June 1911 church services celebrated the coronation of George V. Here the procession of dignitaries, army and (on the left) fire brigade passes the Priory railings on its way to Holy Trinity. Calverley Mount in the background, linking Decimus Burton's Parade and Terrace, was occupied at the time by solicitor Robert Gower.

141. Philip Seale's two lodging houses (see plate 32) gradually became a terrace which in 1871 was home for no fewer than 74 children and adults. Sidney Baker's painting of Sion Crescent shows the scene in about 1900. Evidently in need of renovation, the terrace was demolished in 1913 and a forerunner to the Toc H Hall was built on the site in 1921.

142. David Johnson took this photograph on 8 March 1930, 'a few days before alterations commenced'. Johnson became photographer to the Record Section of the Tunbridge Wells Amateur Photographic Association, set up in 1930 in order to photograph buildings before demolition or alteration. Of *Lonsdale Mansions* and the rest of this Mount Pleasant scene, only the ornamental pillar remains to-day.

143. This lady, photographed by David Johnson in about 1915, was the daughter of James Burrows who is credited with invention of Tunbridge Ware of the inlaid mosaic type. A teacher of drawing and painting, and an artist and poetess, she married George Turner, the deaf and dumb son of a Chafford Mill papermaker, who became a skilled wood and metal worker and photographer. They lived in Poona Road.

144.   A note on the back of this photograph reads, '4 August 1914. C. Squadron, West Kent Yeomanry assembled in their drill hall, the Corn Exchange, Pantiles, before leaving for Maidstone'. From here they marched past cheering, singing crowds to the Central Station. Compare the Corn Exchange now (plate 165).

145.   Robert Gower, the solicitor of Calverley Mount (see plate 140), became mayor in 1917, was knighted in 1919 and entered Parliament in 1924. The *Advertiser*'s cartoon of June 1923 followed a Council debate when Sir Robert opposed the expenditure of ratepayers' money on the Calverley Grounds band pavilion. A pity the Council could not foretell the future (see plate 159)!

"UNDER THE GREENWOOD BOUGH"
OR "SIR ROBERT AND HIS MERRY RATEPAYERS"

"THE OWL"

146. The 300-ft. long open air swimming pool in the old reservoir, which had been fed from the Jack Woods Spring and used by John Ward to supply water to the Calverley development, opened in 1873 and closed during World War Two. The waterworks site, with another four acres given by John Stone-Wigg in 1877, became the Grosvenor Recreation Ground.

147. The General Hospital in the Grosvenor Road (see plate 95) had become increasingly cramped and when Great Culverden House with eight acres of land (see plate 83) came on the market in 1926 a new hospital was planned. The foundation stone was laid by the Duchess of York (our present Queen Mother), seen here with the Marquess Camden, on 19 July 1932. The first patients were admitted on 1 August 1934.

148. David Johnson (1862-1945) was born in one of the Stevenson buildings on the London Road, lived as a boy in York Villa (see below) went to King Charles School, ran a photographic business at No. 39 High Street and lived in the Mount Sion area throughout his long life, except for the years 1885-7 when he joined a friend in a photographic business in Chester, Carolina.

149. The Twitten, Frog Lane: one of the town's most photographed views. As can be seen, Johnson left hand-written historical commentaries. He says also that the building at the back left was used by Mr. Peerless, the fellmonger, for storing sheepskins. On the left foreground is Crescent Lodge, built about 1720, and until 1922 part of the Sion House property.

Crescent Lodge on left.

D.J.JOHNSON

Foot path leading from Mt. Sion to Little Mount Sion. House in centre was my home 1867-1874

150. Fanny Burney, on her visit to the Wells in October 1779, saw 'two or three dirty little lanes, much like dirty little lanes in other places'. Frog Lane was probably one of them, but is now a tourist attraction. The *spalls* (split stones), not *cobbles* (whole stones), appear to be unique to the town, and Frog Lane is the last to be so surfaced. The lane was called Frog Lane until the later 19th century, when it became Murray Road on account of Murray House School at the top. Recently the old name has been reinstated. The stables and coach-houses of Mount Sion lodging houses used to open onto the lane and it is said that 'frog' refers to a kind of brake to hold carriages on a slope. On the left is the corner of York Villa (see plate 148), Frog Cottage, some former stables, and the chimneys and roof of Murray House (see plate 65). On the right is Caxton Cottage.

151. Fairlawn House was started in 1690 as a lodging house by Thomas Scoones (grandfather of the first lawyer Scoones). It became the Girls' High School from 1883 to 1900, and the Eye and Ear Hospital in 1900. In 1789 it was the scene of the attempted abduction of the heiress, Ann Jeffery. This Johnson photograph shows it just after the patients had left for the new hospital in 1934.

152. In 1936 the Literary Society held a Centenary Exhibition at their rooms in No. 32 The Pantiles, later demolished (see plate 153). Prominently displayed is the Beau Nash portrait (see plate 50), together with paintings, maps and photographs, probably by the 'Record Section'. Johnson's obituary mentioned his hope that his photographs and commentaries might be displayed in the 'new' Town Hall.

153. This 1937 Johnson photograph shows the back of Nos. 30-6, with the Library and Reading Room, where the 1936 Exhibition was held, advertising its presence ('Entrance 32, The Pantiles') above the Southern Railway signpost.

154. It is often thought that the shops in the centre of this 1937 Johnson photograph were bombed during the war and that is why a garden, beloved of many, took their place until recently. In truth disrepair caused demolition. They formed part of the Walks Estate and have been 'restored' by the developer who bought out the successors to the 1739 shareholders in 1985.

155. This 1930s' aerial view of the town centre shows, bottom right, Decimus Burton's Parade and part of the Terrace; the gardens behind with the swimming pool where the mews were; top left, part of the old General Hospital; and top centre the huddle of buildings, including the old gas works site, now being developed as the Royal Victoria shopping mall.

156.   This prize-winning picture from local photographer S. K. Lazell has captured the present-day atmosphere of cricket on the 'Upper Ground'; but it has not always been so peaceful. Until the early 19th century the race course ran across the field and the winning post and paddock were nearby. County and international cricket was seen until the Nevill Ground opened in 1898.

157.   Calverley Park and Grounds were created from a scattered ownership of fields by William Lushington during the years between his purchase of Great Mount Pleasant House (briefly named Lushington House) in 1819 and his death in 1824, following which John Ward bought the estate. The house, now the *Calverley Hotel*, can be seen in the background on the left.

158.   Danger! Vandals at work! Part of Decimus Burton's Calverley Terrace is loaded for transportation, while ruins loom behind the heavy machinery. The tall chimney is that of the swimming pool boilerhouse and identifies the building under demolition. The one on the right (Nos. 9 and 10) is the sole survivor today. This photograph was taken in 1938-9.

159.   The Calverley Grounds pavilion and bandstand were built in 1926 in the park created from part of the grounds of the *Calverley Hotel* in 1920. The occasion which prompted this dramatic night photograph is not known. The pavilion was one of the few casualties of the war, being hit by incendiaries from a lone raider on 30 August 1940.

160.   Art School principal E. Owen Jennings, R.W.S., A.R.E., A.R.C.A., drew the air raid shelter in the Sand Caves under the Common in April 1941. The caves are said to link with the wine vaults on Mount Ephraim. There are many stories of tunnels under the Common but perhaps these caves, used for quarrying sand (see plate 77), lie behind most such stories.

The Post-War Period: 1945-90

161. Decimus Burton's Market Place, seen here shored-up before demolition in 1959, was used as the Art School when the Council moved into the new Town Hall. Together with the *Camden Inn*, whence after a good dinner a procession set forth in 1864 to celebrate Dr. Webber's discomfiture, it was replaced by the National Provident offices and ground-floor supermarket.

162. This picture should be compared with Nos. 153-4 and 166. This is the garden which was created to fill the gap in the Pantiles left by the demolition of Nos 30-6. Beyond the colonnade is the fishmarket and the *Duke of York*.

163. This 1959 aerial view shows, top left, the Central Station, and, top centre, the Grove, to the right of which are the houses which replaced Grecian Villa. To the left of the Grove are the houses which replaced the Grove Houses and below the Grove is Mount Sion with three houses since demolished (Murray House, Eden House and Walmer House). Bottom right are Warwick Park and the Frant Road; and bottom centre, the Pantiles showing the 'old' Assembly (Auction) Rooms and Corn Exchange and the Pantiles garden.

164. In less congested days Calverley Road used to be lined every day with market stalls; since 1984 the creation of the town's second pedestrian precinct (the Pantiles is, of course, the first) has brought back the shoppers on foot, if not the street market. In the background is the N.P.I. building (see plate 161) and beyond that Burton's Calverley Place (see plate 82).

165. The condition of the buildings on the Sussex side of the Pantiles had long given cause for concern. In 1985 the Council approved a scheme by developers Speyhawk to include a new auction room, a heritage museum and a food hall which, as can be seen, has been created from Sarah Baker's old theatre, later the Corn Exchange.

166. Compare this photograph of the new houses and shops built on the Pantiles garden site with those shown in plate 154, which were there before the garden. The new building consists of four shops and nine flats.

167. On the right is the Meadow Road multi-storey car park, for which the surviving 1904 wing of the old hospital was recently demolished; ahead tower the cranes of the latest and most ambitious shopping development in the town, Royal Victoria Place, due for completion in 1992.

168.   If life in the 1990s becomes too hectic, we can now return to the year 1740 and a meticulous recreation of 'A Day at the Wells', housed in the old Sussex Assembly Rooms on the Pantiles. In the foreground of this scene two gentlemen are engaged in play on an E and O table, while in the background Beau Nash keeps an eye on the dancing and talks to a lady with an ear-trumpet.

Tunbridge Wells humbly Dedicated

Mount Ephraim

Thompson

Mr Kents

Cloister Tavern

High House

Mortons

T. Badslade Delin:

Uper Walk

Lower Walk